A MORNING
WITHOUT CLOUDS

A MORNING
WITHOUT CLOUDS

HAROLD GASTER

JONATHAN CAPE

THIRTY BEDFORD SQUARE LONDON

First published 1981
© 1981 by Harold Gaster

Jonathan Cape Ltd, 30 Bedford Square, London WC1

British Library Cataloguing in Publication Data

Gaster, Harold
A Morning without Clouds.
1. England – Social life and customs – 20th century
I. Title
942.083'092'4   DA566.4

ISBN 0-224-01964-3

Phototypeset in Linotron 202 Plantin by
Western Printing Services Ltd, Bristol
Printed by Butler & Tanner Ltd,
Frome and London

To the three most important women in my life,
BIRGIT, my wife, JENNIFER, my daughter,
and EMILY, my granddaughter,
I dedicate this little book with love.

Contents

Acknowledgment

I would like to thank Faber & Faber Ltd for permission to quote from George Ewart Evans, *The Days that We Have Seen* (1975).

'As the light of the morning, when the sun riseth, even a morning without clouds; as the tender grass springing out of the earth by clear shining after rain.'

2 Samuel 23: 4

'Certainly Adam in Paradise had not more sweet and curious apprehensions of the world, than I when I was a child.'

THOMAS TRAHERNE

A Morning without Clouds

THERE are times when something, some happening, I hardly know what, will bring about in me a peculiar state of mind. It may happen when I am reading, or listening to music, or perhaps when I am just sitting and looking into the fire. But whatever the cause may be there will flash upon my mind, or upon my mind's eye, a picture from the past, the image of some event or occasion; and when it occurs the picture is so clear and bright that it is like a landscape in a Flemish miniature, a small bright picture seen as in a crystal.

It occurred to me today; and I have resolved that I will try to capture these small bright visions from the past, so that I may keep them like a casket of jewels which I may bring out and enjoy when the mood arises.

Suffolk

I am thinking of myself now as a small boy. I am staying in a house in Suffolk – a long, low, white house. It was a long while ago. I know that, for I remember a servant girl being in a great fright because, she said, 'They say it's the Kaiser's birthday tomorrow and "they" are coming to kill us all.'

But it is not the First World War or the Kaiser that I remember, although these are mixed up with my memories. I remember, for instance, being taken to see the 'volunteers' drilling on the village green after morning church, the Rector among them. Looking back now over all the years between I see a rather clumsy, awkward lot of men, 'old 'uns' left behind by the young men at the Front. They are marching and presenting arms in unsuitable civilian clothes under the bawling instruction of an army sergeant. I was a very small boy and I was never quite sure whether it was a show or what it was.

Something which probably sounds very odd to people today, but which loomed large in the lives of country people in those days and even, to a surprising degree, in the lives of some townsfolk, was the commandeering of the horses. I can only write of what I saw or heard as a small boy. I was told that men from the army would arrive to take the horses from the farm wagons, from the very ploughs, or even, I was assured, from a trap or a cart on the road. I have a dim memory of having seen this happen. To a small farmer or a tradesman relying on his one horse, this could be a very serious matter, and indeed a very sad one, for a horse and a dog were companions to a man who lived and worked with them every day of the week.

But there are other memories. In Suffolk I used to go to the bakehouse, which was not far from the church, up by the village green. And there, in my childish memory, was a woman with a white apron and floury arms, and also a strong smell of yeasty dough, which was 'rising' in wooden troughs. No one who has known the warmth and smell of an old-fashioned bakehouse can ever forget it, or the peculiar sense of comfort associated with it. There was a man who used to open the door of a cavernous brick oven, into which he slid a long-handled peel to bring out batches of hot bread and small cakes. Oh, the smell and the feel of those warm, crusty loaves! I was occasionally given one of the little cakes, and the taste of it, warm from the oven with a slightly crunchy crust, is as real today as when I ate it.

The house we stayed in looked down towards the railway, not far from the little country station. Sometimes long strings of cattle trucks would be waiting on the line, and I would see bullocks and sheep poking their heads through the bars and lowing or baa-ing. The little station was usually quiet. One might sit on a bench on the platform with the sun shining warm and bright, with no sound but two which have become increasingly rare. One was the clanking rattle of milk cans, tall ones that one seldom sees now. A porter would skilfully roll these along, using a spinning action, with his hands at the top, and holding the can at an angle so that it rolled along on its rim at the base. The other was the peculiar, sleepy, 'Chiff! Chuff!' of a small country steam engine standing in a siding. As I listen to these sounds in my mind now I am acutely aware of the quiet countryside stretching away on all sides, and the white dusty lane going away between the hedges.

Beyond the railway line were low-lying water meadows with a watermill and a weir; a path ran along the river bank with stiles between the meadows. By the river grew giant bulrushes with velvety brown heads which showed a white fluffy pith if you pulled them to pieces. There must have been a bridge over the river, for I remember a lane which crossed it and climbed up a hill between high banks, on which grew hips and haws and great masses of old man's beard. In the ploughlands were peewits and partridges – there were often partridges, or a pheasant, or perhaps a hare, hanging in the larder of the house.

It was up this lane that I went to see my first meet of hounds, quite a long walk for a small boy of several miles each way. There were no cars cluttering up the countryside in those days, farmers and grander folk in pink arrived on horseback from all directions, with the followers on foot or in pony traps, and the hounds jostling, with their twinkling sterns and their deep, baying voices. Occasionally if people came from a distance they would arrive on a little local train, bringing their horses in a railway horse-box.

I was given a small patch of garden, quite a tiny patch, but it was my own; and there I had some primroses and violets and a real strawberry plant. To this day nothing quite equals the acute pleasure of seeing the new crinkled leaves of the primroses grow, followed by the little pointed buds which burst to reveal tightly rolled pale yellow flowers; and finally the pale, exquisite flower itself.

A number of memories come back to me as I think of the house. I liked to peep into the larder, where there were many things beside the partridges and other game. In those days refrigerators or deep-freeze chests were virtually unknown. The kind of larder I remember was a cross between a large

cupboard and a small room. It probably had a floor of tiles or
red brick, and the walls and ceiling were whitewashed. In an old
house there would be a deep-set window in the thickness of the
wall, covered on the outside with perforated zinc and on the
inside with white muslin stretched on a wooden frame. It was
on the north side of the house so that no sun could shine in.
Through the gauze one could see a dim, hazy view of the
garden, and if anyone passed by the crunching of their feet was
accompanied by a half-shadow, half-reflection, which moved
across the ceiling in the opposite direction to that of the walker.
Hanging from hooks and nails in the ceiling were poultry or
game, and bunches of herbs – parsley, mint, chives, thyme,
sage – and of onions and shallots. Among these were fly-papers
like long sticky tongues. The walls were lined with shelves, on
which were rows of pots filled with different-coloured jams.
raspberry, gooseberry, red or yellow plum; lower down were
larger jars made of glass or glazed earthenware which held
pickled onions and shallots in vinegar. These pots were covered
with taut parchment caps tied with white string, each one with
its label. All were bright and shining with little, gleaming
highlights. On other shelves were cheeses wrapped in muslin or
under china covers shaped like a wedge of cheese. On the floor
stood earthenware crocks in which beans were laid down in salt
or eggs in waterglass. From the larder came cool air in hot
weather and a wonderful smell compounded of herbs, cheese,
vinegar and other things. I have always loved larders and store-
cupboards, partly because of the actual beauty of their con-
tents, partly because of the sense one had of provisions stored
up against the winter. One of the scenes that I always liked in
The Wind in the Willows was at Badger's house in the Wild
Wood. Outside were snow, rain and cold. Inside old grey
Badger sat in his high-backed chair in dressing-gown and slip-
pers, warm and sleepy by the fireside, conscious of his store of
good things hoarded against the winter.

Other memories are clear. In the kitchen was a row of copper
saucepans ranging from large to small. They were kept clean
and polished, and I remember their brightness. As was common in country houses in those days, the cooking was done on
a wood-burning range and the house was lit by lamps and

candles. It was common to see a row of candlesticks on a dresser or on the kitchen table, and at bedtime one carried one's lighted candle upstairs, where it was placed on a table or chest-of-drawers with a box of matches beside it. In such houses, before the coming of electricity or gas, there was a special smell compounded of wood smoke, paraffin and candle wax, and when the candle was snuffed or blown out when one got into bed the smell of hot candle grease mixed with drowsiness before sleep came. In the parlour, when the blue dusk of evening was gathering over the water meadows, the lamp would be lit. It was a round lamp, which stood on the table and had two wicks, which were trimmed and turned up a little and then lit with a paper spill. We used to make these spills from long strips of paper, and they stood in a pot on the mantelpiece. Next a glass chimney was fitted over the flames so that they burned bright and clear with no smoke; and finally a round glass globe with a pattern on it was lowered over the chimney, often striking it with a small 'clink!' As the globe was lowered into position a pattern of golden stars spread across the ceiling. From the warm yellow lamplight of the parlour the garden and the world outside became an intense, beautiful blue until the curtains were drawn and they were shut out.

At that time many ladies were doing 'war work' in their houses. Some knitted socks and mufflers, others made shirts or rolled strips of linen for use as bandages. There was a popular song called 'Sister Susie's Sewing Shirts for Soldiers':

> But the soldiers wrote epistles,
> Said they'd rather sleep on thistles,
> Than the saucy, soft, short, silky shirts
> That Sister Susie sewed.

They used to crochet pads made of thick wool for putting under the saddles of army horses to prevent saddle sores. I learned to crochet and made some of these myself; though possibly the horses' opinions of my handiwork echoed those of the soldiers who wore Sister Susie's shirts.

Ladies also indulged in various arts and crafts. One did 'pen-painting', she used to make table-centres of black velvet, decorated with raised patterns of roses and leaves of some kind of stiff pigment put on with a pen. They were greatly admired.

We used to bath in front of the fire in the kitchen, in a wide, shallow, enamelled bath exactly like a frying pan. These baths which, when not in use, would hang or stand against a wall in the wash-house, were of two kinds — the wide shallow ones, and a deeper sort with a tall back and flat pieces at the sides to put the soap on. They had to be carried in and filled from a large pot or kettle on the range. After the bath they were emptied, wiped out and hung up once again.

Occasionally we went to visit a farm some miles away, making the journey in a pony trap. The farm belonged to a son and daughter-in-law of the family who owned the house in Suffolk. They had a boy about the same age as I was and I remember a smaller child. Here life was very free. There was a stackyard where we used to play, sometimes climbing up the stacks and sliding off them on to piles of loose straw; or we would help to collect the eggs, which meant searching in stables, haylofts and dark corners under haystacks, or in hedge bottoms or any place where the wandering hens might decide to lay. Sometimes we went round after dusk with a sparrow net and a lantern, to catch sparrows before they could damage the stack. The net was stretched between two long poles. Two men held it open like a banner in a procession and it was placed against an ivy-covered wall. The sparrows, disturbed by the net and the light of the lantern, attempted to fly out and were caught.

Perhaps my most vivid memory is of the threshing, which was a tremendous business. Men would arrive with one of the old threshing machines which went from farm to farm, unless the farmer was in a large way and could afford to buy his own. It was driven by a belt from an old-fashioned steam traction engine. I can never hear such a sound even now without recapturing that scene — a steady droning hum with the puffing of the engine and the belt, driven by a large wheel, flying between the thresher and the engine.

It was a sound which was common in any corn-growing district after harvest time; one could hear the drone of the machine across the fields, a seasonal sound going with the autumn and the late sunshine. The air was full of corn-smelling dust, as the men pitched the sheaves from the corn ricks and fed them into the thresher; and in all directions as the stacks were unbuilt ran rats and mice — hundreds of them as it seemed to me — and they were pursued by small boys, among them myself, who killed them with sticks, and by innumerable dogs. I remember one boy shouting in the local dialect, 'Meece! Meece!' Strangely enough no feeling of brutality comes to me from that scene — I was only a small boy — but it was part of the farm life along with the ducks on the pond, the partridges and peewits in the ploughland and the smell of straw and corn in the sunshine.

One more memory — a piece of dialect which I learned and which must be spoken with a long drawl.

'Wheer b'ye gooen' bor?' 'Arter fa-a-a-gots.' 'Yew stop theer till ah coom back and ah'l 'elp yer dra-a-ag 'em!'

Sussex

In some men's lives there comes a time which may be long or short; its length is irrelevant, what matters is its intensity. And such a time may be so intense as to colour the whole of a man's future life; to remain an inexhaustible source of strength. One may think of Samuel Palmer. Everything that mattered to him as a creative artist happened in the seven years he lived at Shoreham. He lived to be an old man; and as an old man he looked back to 'that first flush of summer splendour which so enchanted me at Shoreham'.

So it is with me. I feel increasingly that the whole of my life as a painter has been conditioned by the time I spent in Sussex as a boy. This is something which can never die and never fail me. I find my thoughts turning back more and more to those days, recapturing experiences which are the stuff of my life, without which I could never have become the kind of painter that I am.

We lived in a four-roomed cottage on the side of a steep hill, not just because of poverty (although we were poor enough) but because of peculiar circumstances.

The cottage stood at the top of a strip of ground, about half an acre in extent, which ran parallel with the road and was separated from it by a hedge. In front of the cottage was a little patch of flower garden with a brick path from the door to the garden gate. The rest of the strip was a vegetable garden with a couple of apple trees and, at the bottom, a piece of rough grass where we kept chickens. As you faced the cottage from the road a path on the right-hand side went round to the back, where there were two pigsties and a privy. On the opposite side another path led to a small outbuilding, which contained the domed top of the brick oven. These ovens were common and in regular use in many houses for the weekly bake. The space above the oven was large enough to make a kind of den, and I often used to sit there reading on a wet day in summer.

In the little front garden were flowers – wallflowers, forget-me-nots, violets, some 'tots' of primroses and a brilliant pink shamrock which opened out in a blaze of colour when the sun shone and closed when it was dull. There was a bush of 'old man' by the gate, which had a lovely aromatic smell if you pinched it; and against the walls of the cottage, in the cracks between the bricks of the path, grew a little yellow flower with a leaf rather like maiden-hair fern. It was common in all the cottage gardens, and to me is inseparable from that district. Between us and the garden above us, which belonged to the shop, was a rough wall of earth and stones topped with a mass of bramble and ivy.

Outside the gate the road, rough, white and stony in those days, climbed steeply to the right towards the village and fell away as steeply to the left. Opposite was an orchard and a grassy bank which shone with the greenish light of glow-worms on summer nights. A little up the hill, on the opposite side, a double cottage stood back from the road looking across the valley. In the further one lived two old ladies who were sisters, in the nearer one a family consisting of father, mother and a small boy. Further up the hill on the same side was a stable covered with climbing roses, where the people at the shop kept their horses, and a cart hole, which was an open-ended shed for their trap and farm carts. Whenever I think of this stable I hear the clear ringing song of many chaffinches, the place seemed to be full of them. Is it my fancy or was there a special clarity in their songs, a kind of local dialect?

Further up still, on our side of the road, was a small square of land set back from the road, where the little shop stood. On the left of the square as you entered it was another cottage, high on a bank and approached by some steps. This was occupied by a family whom I will call Cobble. The shop was owned by an old man whom I will call Farmer, and run by his son, grandson and niece, who between them managed the shop, the bakehouse, and a farm. In fact almost everyone in the immediate neighbourhood was a Farmer, a Cobble or a Cartwright – though these are not their actual names – and I never fathomed out their complex relationships.

I can still remember every inch of the road to the village. After the shop and the stable it rose steeply for a short way. On the left just here was a little hollow, almost a half circle, cut into a meadow which was higher than the road. It was sheltered and in the spring the whole of the grassy bank was studded with primroses. After the steep section the road levelled out and then divided into two, the left fork going up hill to the village proper, the right to a lower or lesser part of the village. On the left just before the fork was a small barn made of heavy timbers, very mossy and green; I remember the white flash of a tree split into two during a thunderstorm up against the park wall. On the right were two cottages with gardens full of flowers. In the triangle between the two roads and facing one as one approached the fork stood a house behind yew hedges clipped in the likeness of a cock and a hen. It was known as the 'Cock and Hen House'. I cannot remember the people who lived there except for a dimly seen elderly figure; the whole house and garden were hidden, withdrawn behind the high clipped hedge. But sometimes if we stood outside the gate there would be a thump! thump! on the road and two or three apples would land beside us. They were old-fashioned green apples, turning yellow as they ripened. The house and its owners remain a mystery in my mind because they were so hidden by the tall hedges.

From here up to the village on the left-hand side of the road ran the wall of the park, a stone wall which must have been very long, for as far as I remember it enclosed most of the park. On the right there was a spinney and after that fields till one reached the top of the hill. Here another road went downhill to the right past the Rectory, the blacksmith's and a small inn. But straight ahead lay the village, the church and the Squire's house.

In the opposite direction from our gate the road plunged steeply down into the valley round a couple of sharp bends. Farm lads going home in the evening would rush by on their bicycles ringing their bells furiously. The opposite side of the valley was a wooded hill, indeed a forest of some extent, for we lived in a heavily wooded district. At the bottom of the hill the road ran quite level along the valley with the wooded hill on the left and, on the right, meadowland with a small stream and a farm. Down in the hollow facing the woods was a collection of cottages inhabited by some Cobbles, Farmers and Cartwrights. A Mrs Farmer, daughter-in-law of the old man at the shop, lived here. To my childish eyes she was so broad as to appear almost square. She had a loud voice and florid face, and a very good heart. I often saw her pushing a bicycle, but I cannot imagine that she can ever have ridden it. There was another woman called Cobble, a young woman with a shrill, penetrating voice. She had a boy called Alfie, and we could hear her from our cottage calling 'Al-*fee*! Al-*fee*!'

One of my pleasantest memories is of the cottages, sometimes single, sometimes two together, sometimes in small rows. Some were built of stone, some of brick with hung tiles of a warm earthy red. Some were of wood tarred black. Many belonged to the estate, and the doors and windows were painted a pale buff or stone colour. Every cottage had its garden, its faggot pile, its water butt. Usually there was a strip of garden between the cottage and the road, with a path, probably of worn bricks, from the garden gate to the door. On either side of the path were vegetables – potatoes, cabbages, peas, beans, carrots, lettuces, onions – all in straight rows, with the earthed-up potatoes, the pale green of lettuces, the blue-green and pearly white of onions, the feathery tops of carrots, the rows of peas and beans with the brushy sticks of the peas and the tall poles of the bean rows with red flowers and vine-like leaves, all contrasting with a border of currant and gooseberry bushes and flowers on either side of the path. In the spring there were snowdrops, crocuses, daffodils, and patches of primroses and wallflowers. Later came the roses, old-fashioned cabbage and moss roses, less showy than their modern relations but with a fragrance that is rare today. The little moss rose may not be an exhibition flower but to me it is more lovely than any overblown prize-winner, with a kind of cottage charm that nothing can replace. There were rosemary and mint, thyme and deep-green parsley and blue-green sage, sweet-williams, clove-scented pinks and stocks, and rows of sweet-peas that perfumed the whole air. There were bushes of old man and bright golden marigolds, pink and freckled daisies and monk's hood and golden rod. The little yellow flower that grew against our cottage wall was to be seen everywhere.

The cottage walls, especially those facing south, were covered with pear trees and victoria plums. There is nothing quite like a ripe, sweet victoria plum warm with the sun, picked and eaten with the bloom on it, straight from a cottage wall; often early summer apples would lie, bright red among wet grass and beds of mint, sage and thyme; and, to me, the smell of the mint and other herbs is part of the smell and taste of the apples. How different were the old gnarled, twisted trees, some half-recumbent or propped with poles, grey and green and silver with lichen and moss, from the straight, well-ordered rows of the commercial orchard. These little bits of orchard with their long grass, their cow-parsley, cuckoo flowers and buttercups, their coops of chicks and ducklings, their children and kittens playing in the sun, were all part of the scene. Beside the cottage there was usually a wood-shed and in the winter a pyramid of bean poles ready for summer use; and there would be a faggot pile and a privy, probably hidden by a lilac bush or an elderberry or smothered in ivy or creeper. As the summer advanced and the gooseberries and currants ripened, the bushes were covered with pieces of old Nottingham-lace curtains to keep off the birds.

Many people today have bought and repaired old country houses and cottages. They have saved them from destruction and decay; they have created beautiful gardens. But I must be allowed a certain feeling of regret when I think that those old cottages were the homes of genuine country people. If one has known farms where real farming families lived; cottages which were the homes of country folk, many of whom had scarcely seen a town in their lives unless it was on a visit to a little market town; it seems to me that one must regret the passing of that old rural life. I still know gardens in out-of-the-way places which are like those which I have attempted to describe, but they are growing fewer, as are the people who lived in them. It seems to me that these people were the last inheritors of a rural tradition which went back hundreds of years. They were, for me, involved in a kind of dual creation. They created the countryside and the countryside created them. Two major wars, the coming of the motor car, the aeroplane, the radio and television have changed the rural life that I knew more than it had changed in hundreds of years. I often find young people today to whom the Second World War is something of which they have read or heard. Figures like Churchill, Hitler, Montgomery and Rommel are as far off to them as Wellington and Napoleon were to me. If I appear to look back with unreal nostalgia, remember that I recollect quite clearly England and the English countryside before the First World War. I have ridden beside my nurse in a horse bus; I have ridden in a handsom cab; when I was a small boy one would see four-wheeled 'growlers' outside any of the larger railway stations, and horse traffic was common in towns and cities. The English countryside stretched clean and bright and silent, save for 'natural' noises, with deep leafy lanes and white stony roads and no such thing as a motorway.

It is this England from which anything good that I have done as a painter has sprung.

Where there were several cottages together there was often a pump or well. One such well was beside the road a quarter of a mile or so above our cottage. We used to open the wooden trap and lie on our stomachs, peering down at the small circle of water infinitely far away, and we would drop a stone in to make ripples. Over the well was a roller on struts with a chain and a double handle, one at each end of the roller, so that two people could wind the bucket up. You hooked your bucket on an iron hook with a spring catch and then let it fall, the handles of the windlass going faster and faster until the bucket struck the water with a hollow, echoing smack. The art then was to get it under the water, not just floating on the top, which needed a deft jerk of the chain; and then began the long haul up, with the windlass making a sound like the screeching of a guinea-fowl. Mostly the men would fetch the water, carrying two buckets at a time slung at each end of a wooden yoke which fitted across their shoulders. One of these yokes hung in the kitchen or scullery of almost every cottage. The men would generally draw enough in the evening to last the next day, and the buckets would stand on the brick floor of the scullery where it was cool, the water being ladled out as it was required with a round iron dipper on a wooden handle. I have often drunk from such a dipper, not putting my mouth to the edge but pursing it up and sucking in the water, cold from the well in the hottest weather, and tasting faintly of iron from the dipper.

We got most of our drinking water from a pump up by the shop. It tasted strongly of iron as did much of the local water. Many brooks had a reddish foam and left a rusty deposit on the banks. Washing water was caught in a wooden butt from the roof, and one of the sounds in wet weather, especially when all was still at night, was the gurgling of the rain-water as it rushed out of the pipe into the butt. This water was soft and kind to the face and smelt of rain and leaves. Often in the summer one could watch the 'water boatmen', a kind of beetle with oars, skimming on the surface or diving below.

The very best drinking water, indeed the loveliest water I have ever known, so sweet and clear and full of life, came from a spring at the bottom of the hill. It was collected in a brick chamber like a grotto, with walls on three sides and a roof or canopy. It was clear and bright as crystal; so cold and sweet that one would drink for the pleasure of it. To suck up such water, straight from the spring, without the intervention of a cup or glass, was to drink living water. The brickwork of the tank was a pleasant warm red, worn by the action of the water; it was covered with mosses like pin-cushions and patterned with orange, grey and silver lichens, and little ferns grew in the crevices. Stones that had fallen in lay on the bottom, bright as precious stones. I have often lain on my front in hot weather with my face in the water, the whole moving and trembling in the golden light of the sun, the sound of running water in my ears.

Near to this spring was a gate into the woods, some miles of woodland in which much of my time was spent. Among my earliest memories of these woods is a sound which it is hard to imagine if one has never heard it, impossible to forget if one has. One is tempted to use a cliché – it was like the sound of distant thunder. It was not; it was like nothing but itself – the distant gunfire from Flanders. There were times when it was loud and insistent, but often it seemed more of a movement than a sound, a trembling and pulsing of the air. As a small boy I cannot claim that I realized the implications of this low, constant mutter; but when I had been alone for some time in the woods the sound would suddenly break through so that I became aware of it, and I would take to my heels and run for home.

While a more sombre mood is on me I will mention one more such event. This did not happen in the woods but while I was at boarding school, and it must have been at about the same time. I was coming round the school by the paddock where we small boys played cricket and football and where the fives courts stood. It was a murky, purplish evening in autumn with a creeping haze and, above, the fading afterglow in the sky. Just above a bank of cloud, low over the horizon, I saw an enormous black aeroplane. It hardly seemed to move but hung over the landscape like an evil monster, a reincarnation of the dragons of ancient times; and as it hung there from its engine came a low droning, throbbing sound like the growling of a beast. It seemed to me then, and seems now as I look back, the personification of evil. Am I recreating and enlarging this experience in the light of future events? I think not. This evil presence stayed with me for days, remained with me like the looming crag seen by Wordsworth when he was a boy.

This is perhaps a suitable place to mention one more event; a small thing, perhaps, yet one that I can never forget. There were, at that time, a number of Danish forestry workers engaged in cutting timber in the woods. Normally this timber was used for pit props, but I was told that at this time it went to Flanders for building trenches.

Up above the 'Cock and Hen House' a wooded hollow lay back from the road, and on my way home from the village one day I came on a group of Danes at work there. They were felling a tree. I must make it plain that I stood watching them in idle curiosity as any small boy might and I was quite unprepared for what followed. As I watched, the tree began to tremble all over its length and then very slowly it began to fall. The momentum increased until it went over with a crashing roar and lay full length upon the ground. I was overpowered by such an extraordinary feeling of sadness that the tears came into my eyes; and this sadness hung upon me for days afterwards. To this day I can never see a fine tree fall without a recurrence of that sadness, more conscious now, perhaps, of a sense of irreparable loss as though life itself had become poorer.

The Woods

As I write this it is Thomas-tide, and we are having a spell of mild cloudy weather such as is often associated with this time of year before Christmas. It is the kind of weather when firelight and lamplight take on a new golden intensity; when a candle burning in a cottage window or a stable lantern in a cowshed at milking time in the soft winter dusk are like symbols of domestic peace and security. It is a time when I often find myself in a contemplative state of mind, when I am acutely aware of such things.

I am now in my seventies. For nearly half a century I have lived in a thatched cottage in Warwickshire, a beautiful old cottage built of Cotswold stone, with a garden in front where I grow old-fashioned cottage flowers: the shrub roses which are sweet and scented as roses used to be, sweet-williams, stocks, the old clove-scented pinks, hollyhocks, sweet-peas, lavender, cornflowers and marigolds, at the back is a grass orchard full of apple blossom in spring, a place where silvery-white cow-parsley, buttercups and dandelions and fragrant ground ivy may grow as they used to grow in the lanes and meadows when I was a boy. In my special room, which looks out on to the flower garden, there is an enormous old fireplace where I burn logs. There I may sit, as I sit now, staring into the fire, smelling the wood smoke, and recreating in my mind those bright visions of the past of which I have written.

I find, more and more, that I hark back to those enchanted Sussex days that seem at once so far off and yet so near and acutely remembered. As the dark December days come on it seems, in my memory, that there was the same soft, cloudy weather that we have been having lately. The wooded country-side was all around, low toned, purple and brown and grey under a gentle, soft sky. The brooks and the ditches were full.

Down at the bottom of the hill, where the gate led into the woods, the stream was rushing under the bridge and little rivulets were pouring down the steep woodland tracks, stirring up the yellow clay in small cataracts and forming pools of water in the long, rain-filled cart ruts. These were quite unlike the ruts left by tractors, which seem merely destructive, at enmity with the woods. The deep ruts made by the wagons and the ground poached and pitted by the great shaggy feet of the draught-horses were part of the scene: as were the men – each with a sack over his shoulders in wet weather, his corduroy trousers hitched up below his knees with a strap or a band of straw, his battered cap or felt hat, his large hob-nailed boots – plodding through the wet woods alongside the horses.

As I penetrated further into the woods I was in a world of browns and purples, greys and soft greens. The bracken glowed in the damp air, a deep, almost phosphorescent, burnt sienna glow. The birches were silver surmounted by a purple haze of twigs, the pale slender trunks marked with rings and blotches of dark green, purplish brown and black. The beeches towered up against the sky, the colour of elephants, and looking very like elephants with their massive trunks and branches, the acute pencilled beauty of the twigs seen against the grey of the clouds. The coppices of chestnut were black, the ground a damp gold with little touches of acid green in the fallen masses of leaves. The hazels were brownish grey; the alders purple and deep, bottle green; the sycamore pale, olive green and rosy brown. Further off the bare woods were cloudy masses of purple twigs with misted blue-greys, ash colours, browns and yellow-greys among them. The willows and osiers down by the stream were shining yellow rods turning red at the tips, the ancient trunks of the larger trees had long ribs of bark a browner colour, the hollows in a pollarded tree were deep peaty brown streaked with a colour that was near russet and copper.

The stream was no longer the quiet, almost soundless stream of summer with silver ripples and breaks and deep silent pools: now it was a full, rushing, swelling volume of water, made opaque by the burden of clay which it swept along, driving masses of sodden leaves on to the small sandy beaches; foaming and rushing where boulders or a fallen log made an obstruction; overflowing its banks in pools and sheets of water where the land was flat. The rushes were bent double, sere and yellow and stained with brown; and where a branch hung low it was half submerged, bending and thrashing with the force of the current.

How many hours, how many days, have I spent beside this stream, absorbed into its full winter life so that I forgot time and all other things. I would find a floating log and launch it out into the stream, piloting it with a long hazel rod, steering it past submerged roots or stones, and guiding it into the main stream of a rapid so that it shot down the channel with a rearing plunge to sink out of sight and then to reappear on its mad course among the waves and whirlpools lower down.

Further on was an old ruined mill, and by it the water stretched in a sheet of silver, having abandoned its channel altogether. It was so high that it nearly reached the top of the arches of the bridge and, bursting out the other side, roared down the shute in a torrent of foam and flashing, writhing water. Down below, in stiller water, the leaves, bits of wood and flakes of foam and bubbles swung round and round in miniature whirlpools to shoot out of sight again round a bend by a little cliff.

We made ourselves a truck from a box on wheels, with which we went wooding. We would lug it along the tracks, our feet sucking and sticking in wet yellow clay or slithering when we tried to pull the truck out of the mud, so that we would lie on the ground helpless with laughter and plastered from head to foot with clay. We loaded the truck with sticks and chunks of wood and fir cones so that we could hardly pull it along, and then it was time to go home for tea. We would pile the spoils in the woodshed, scrape as much yellow clay off our shoes and clothes as we could, and clean up before sitting down by the fire with hot cups of tea and toast, which we made against the red embers and covered with dripping and salt, as happy as it is possible for humans to be.

Those winter evenings which we spent by the fire would seem strange to many children today. There was no radio, no television, no raucous noise or blaring 'pop'. We sat on the hearth-rug with our books, the room warm with firelight and yellow lamplight, or if other children were there we played wonderful games: Halma or Snakes and Ladders; Snap; Happy Families; Animal Grab; Head, Body and Lets or Consequences. When bedtime came we climbed the little, steep, wooden stairs to small cottage bedrooms, our way lighted with a candle. One part of going to bed was to fetch the candlesticks, strike a match, which made a faint sulphurous smell, and hold the flame against the wick of the candle, which changed with the heat from a hard, bent stalk, rather like a mouse's tail, to a soft, limp thing before it caught and then burned in a steady yellow flame.

Upstairs the candlestick stood on the chest-of-drawers or a small table. I would lie in bed, warm and comfortable, with the flame of the candle burning clear gold with a blue centre, scarcely moving in the still air of the room and casting strange shadows of chairs, washstand and towel horse on the walls, until someone came in, blew out the light and opened the window. A candle burning in a quiet room produces a hypnotic sense, almost a sense of trance, and a great feeling of comfort and security.

When I was a small boy I was quite often unwell, but my memories of such occasions are not unpleasant. Being in bed with a bad cold or after an attack of croup meant having a fire in the bedroom and books to read. How often have I lain in bed at night, my mind full of enchanting stories, for I read a great deal and when I read I lived in my books; indeed I had a capacity to retreat into a private world. The candle was out but the fire still burned with a gentle murmuring sound, and the firelight danced on the ceiling, casting strange shadows which came and went with the flickering flames, made by the high nursery guard with a brass rail which always stood before the fire. In the morning in winter the candle burned yellow once again and the world outside was a beautiful blue as the daylight increased. I am reminded of Robert Louis Stevenson:

A Morning without Clouds

In winter I get up at night
And dress by yellow candlelight.
In summer just the other way,
I have to go to bed by day.

I have quite often found that the very things which give me such pleasure, bare woods in winter at the dim time of November and December with gentle soft mist or rain, have exactly the opposite effect on other people. I have always loved to wander deep into woodlands, preferably by myself, when they are, as some people appear to feel, melancholy. To me they are not melancholy but extraordinarily beautiful, with low-toned glowing colours, the pungent smells of rotting leaves and the sound of drops falling from the branches of the trees. Another state in nature which affects me in much the same way is a deep fall of snow, which brings a wonderful silence. But although there was not, in those peaceful days, so much to torment lovers of quietness I already loved that peace and I already had a capacity to look and to savour the smell of growing things and to hear small sounds that many people never hear. My times in those woods have stayed with me all my life and I think that I was fortunate, as few people are now, to have seen and known so much which others, coming later, have not seen or known.

After the cold days of January the evenings started to lengthen and the drying winds brought about a change. A great deal of the woodland where we lived was coppice wood, grown for use, yet not regimented or turned into plantations. We had never heard of the Forestry Commission and we would not have understood anyone who spoke of conservation, landscape development, green belts or 'planning'. It was simply the countryside, where country people lived and worked. These people were as much part of the rural scene as the fields and the meadows, the cottages and the barns and the woods themselves. We seldom saw a motor car in those parts; people walked or drove in pony traps and carts, or at the most used a bicycle.

In February the ground began to dry up, a wind, often cold and wintery, blew through the copses of hazel and ash, so that the long slender growth from the stools rattled and clashed together. The twiggy masses of the birches and the hazels were dashed to and fro against the grey skies of early spring. The ashes turned a pale, greenish grey, and the ash buds were dark and sharp against the light. Towards the end of February there would come still evenings with a yellow-grey light in the sky and the loud cheerful songs of thrushes. It was then that we began to see the stirrings of early spring. The honeysuckle bines produced little tongues of green fire, the catkins hung in yellow-green clusters from the hazel boughs. The bright enamelled flowers of the celandines, with their glossy, spade-shaped leaves, began to appear in sheltered places. On some days the pale sunlight slanted down casting a network of thin shadows on the brown leaf mould.

March came, with roaring winds and lashing branches, and the shouting of the storm cocks high in the oak trees. There were sudden sharp showers of hail which stung one's face. Later the bitter winds returned and the hedges, still purple and brown and bare, were covered with the snow of the blackthorn and the thin crying of lambs could be heard in the meadows.

And then suddenly the wind went round to the south-west; there were showers of soft, warm rain and a bloom of growing things lay everywhere. From now on it was one long miracle. The gold of the celandines was joined by the purple-blue of violets; the windflowers came in sheets of frail white flowers with pinkish stems and feathery leaves; and then, best and dearest of all, came the primroses. I cannot think of these now without an ache which is half-pleasure and half-pain, the pain which too great a beauty can cause in humans. First came the crinkled green leaves, next the furled buds, and then the wide-open flowers of that clear ecstatic yellow which no other flower can show. They were everywhere: in patches on the brown leaf mould, on every bank and beneath every hedge. One could pick them by the hundred and there still seemed as many; and one could bunch them in round country bundles surrounded by their own leaves and tied with rushes; or one could simply sit in the spring sunshine and look at them, wondering if any paradise could offer more. If Adam and Eve had had English woods and primroses they would not have bothered about the tree of knowledge.

From now on the season was a pageant. The primroses faded — it was almost good that they should not last too long. Then came the broom and the campions; the bird-cherry and the crab-apple; the brilliant yellow-green flowers of the syca-mores; the patches of green grass speckled with daisies and small yellow buttercups; blue forget-me-nots with golden centres; wild pansies and purple bugle; the intense blue of the bluebells, a carpet beneath the hazels with their sharp green leaves; and, to crown all, companies of foxgloves, spire behind spire of noble flowers, the bells purple-pink and their insides splotched with an exquisite pattern. When they came, and after them, the wild roses festooned every hedge; and then it was summer.

The accompaniment to this lavish display of flowers and new green leaves on every tree and bush was the song of the birds. First was the chiff-chaff, seeming the perfect counterpart to the sharp spiky beauty of the twigs. Then came the willow-wren, trilling from every bush, the sharp song of the whitethroat, the little, cheerful jenny-wren, the swallows skimming across the water by the old mill, the shrill laughing of the yaffle with his 'B.r.r.r.r!' among the trees as he searched for insects, the ringing songs of the chaffinches. The whole wood was alive with birds where all had been so silent; the banks were full of the bobbing, cotton-tailed rabbits, and hunting weasels and stoats; the streams were crowded with water voles and in the denser parts of the wood were the shyer and more secret badgers and foxes. Wherever one looked there were bright eyes, fluttering wings, or the long, craning necks of young birds in their nests, their wide open beaks like yellow fungi. Snakes slithered through the grass or basked in the sun, shrews squeaked and rustled among dead leaves, the darting forms of trout were seen in the brooks, and over all the cuckoo called from early light until the setting of the sun.

The ecstasy of spring was followed by the full sombre quiet of summer. The summer silence of the woods was quite different from that of winter; it was an intense but living stillness full of faint stirrings and rustlings. The birds no longer sang from every branch, but one heard the harsh cries of jays and magpies or the low murmur of myriads of insects. One would come on dark, still pools of water fringed with reeds, and damp, boggy patches where sphagnum moss made soft carpets and white cotton-grass looked weird and luminous. The paths were arched over with so dense a growth that one walked in green gloom on a damp soundless floor, coming out suddenly into a clearing where the hot sunlight blazed down. In much of the wood the bracken grew as high as a small boy, and if one pushed through it felt cold against one's face or hands, and was as thick as a miniature jungle with a smell that always made me think of bananas. The plants in the shady wood were damp and green, with patches of pale fine grasses like hair, but where the hot sun shone in the clearings there was short grass and moss and many plants like purple bugle, wild pansies, scarlet pimpernel and wild strawberries, of which we picked enough to make scarlet-coloured jam. Sometimes in hot sultry weather purple clouds would gather, the thunder would roll and torrents of rain fall; and then the clouds parted and the hot sunshine glittered upon the wet leaves and grasses.

Summer passed. The hazels were loaded with nuts, the ground beneath the oaks was thick with acorns, there were purple-black sloes in the hedges and banks of shining black-berries. Soon it was autumn. The heavy sombre green of late summer underwent a miraculous change with the first frosts. The beeches blazed into an amazing copper-gold, the maples were paler, the oaks a wonderful tawny colour, the ash trees turned a fainter greenish yellow, the hawthorns were bronze with red berries, and whole plantations of larch which had been an incredible green in the spring now turned a sombre yet brilliant ochre. The sky was a milky blue; in the evening trails of mist rose from the damp ground and the owls hooted and screeched beneath the moon. The air was dead still so that the frail cobwebs pearled with dew were motionless; and then suddenly one morning, after a sharp frost, one could stand still in the depth of the woods and hear, on every side, little patter-ing noises as the leaves fell to the ground and lay there in the autumn sunshine, dense and thick, glowing with every shade of gold and bronze and copper and lemon yellow and acid green, with the earth dark, damp brown where it showed between the drifts.

A Morning without Clouds

One night there came a gale out of the south-west; the woods were in an uproar until, miraculously, the tempest passed. It was still and quiet as a pond, every leaf was stripped from the trees and once again it was winter.

'That Sweet Monotony'

WHEN I read over what I have written in these pages I have a feeling that to people whose lives have been more active and complex than mine it may seem that I am remembering a great many trivialities. To me this is not so, for a great part of my life has been made up of just such things. George Eliot has written in *The Mill on the Floss* of the important part such small things play in one's life.

What novelty is worth that sweet monotony where everything is known, and *loved* because it is known.

The wood I walk in on this mild May day, with the young yellow-brown foliage of the oaks between me and the blue sky, the white star-flowers and the blue-eyed speedwell, and the ground ivy at my feet – what grove of tropic palms, what strange ferns or splendid broad-petalled blossoms, could ever thrill such deep and delicate fibres within me as this home-scene? These familiar flowers, these well-remembered bird-notes, this sky, with its fitful brightness, these furrowed and grassy fields, each with a sort of personality given to it by the capricious hedgerows – such things as these are the mother tongue of our imagination, the language that is laden with all the subtle inextricable associations the fleeting hours of our childhood left behind them. Our delight in the sunshine on the deep-bladed grass to-day, might be no more than the faint perception of wearied souls, if it were not for the sunshine and the grass in far-off years, which still live in us, and transform our perception into love.

Hardy writes in a similar vein in *The Woodlanders*. He is writing of the doctor, Fitzpiers, who was such an alien figure in that small, rural world.

> Winter in a solitary house in the country, without society, is tolerable, nay, even enjoyable and delightful, given certain conditions . . . They were present to the lives of Winterborne, Melbury, and Grace; but not to the doctor's. They are old association – an almost exhaustive biographical or historical acquaintance with every object, animate and inanimate, within the observer's horizon. He must know all about those invisible ones of the days gone by, whose feet have traversed the fields which look so grey from his windows; recall whose creaking plough has turned those sods from time to time; whose hands planted the trees that form a crest to the opposite hill; whose horses and hounds have torn through that underwood . . . The spot may have beauty, grandeur, salubrity, convenience; but if it lack memories it will ultimately pall upon him who settles there without opportunity of intercourse with his kind.

I think I could venture to add to this. There are some men and women who have a kind of affinity with rural England, even with parts where they have never been before. It is really this that I mean when I say that some painters are country painters rather than landscape painters.

It is precisely 'that sweet monotony' that I am trying to recall, which is to me the most important possession of my life, for it is often the small things which I remember most clearly.

When I have experienced quite extraordinary pleasure in certain things, or when I have felt a powerful sense of unity with certain places, I have often wondered how much this is due to inherited memories. Why, for instance should agricultural landscape, the forms and rhythms of farming, move me so deeply – so much more profoundly than the drama of wild nature, marvellous though that may be? I have often found that if I have been staying among picturesque or dramatic scenery, when I return again in a rural, farming landscape, I have an extraordinary sense of being where I belong. My father's mother was the daughter of a Sussex farmer near to this very place where I experienced such a sense of belonging. My uncle told me that when his aunt, my grandmother's sister, grew old she had a longing to return to her native place, as an animal may return to its lair to die. A farmer's wife whom I have known for many years, the daughter of an old farming family, said to me, 'It is in the blood.' I believe it is.

It may seem as though I believe that all that was old was good, and all that is new bad. This is not quite true; certainly in a material sense many people are better off than they were. But my great fear is that in concentrating on higher material standards we may lose many things which are, I believe, infinitely precious. This is particularly true of our treatment of this beautiful country in our search for material wealth, for once that countryside is gone I cannot see how it can be replaced; and that loss is too terrible to contemplate.

One day I was talking to a man who was doing some digging for us in the strip of garden beside the road. It had been hot, dry weather and we had just had a thunder shower. A neighbour coming by in his pony trap stopped to talk to the man over the hedge.

'That was a WUNNERFUL good rain!' he called out, 'JUST ABOUT saved the gardens. My peas look lovely!'

It was a small incident; and yet the pleasure on his face, and the cheerful ring in his voice, went so with the freshness in the air after the rain and the new look of life on all growing things that it has stayed with me.

Among my greatest pleasures I would place the coming of the birds in spring, when every bush and hedge rang with song; almost the greatest pleasure lay in the return of the swallows and the martins and the first calling of the cuckoo. I think it is because no other birds, except perhaps the robin, appear to be so intimately related to human life. From the moment when one hears the twitter of the swallow overhead, for the whole summer of his undulating flight and his serene warbling song, a perfect expression of happiness and well-being, he seems to be part of one's life. The swallows in the barn and the martins under the eaves of the cottages have no parallel. It is as though with their coming some benign spirit is with us once more; with their going in the autumn some almost human being has gone.

There is a superstition among some old folk that the martins over the cottage windows are the spirits of those who have lived in the houses. It does not seem to me an extraordinary idea. As for the cuckoo, there is no magic quite like this fluting call in the woods.

The woods in which we spent so much of our time were very extensive. In some parts they consisted of coppices of hazel, chestnut or ash grown for a variety of uses and cut at regular intervals. They were used for hurdles, fencing, hop-poles and much else. Because they were cut regularly when they reached a certain size which depended on the kind of wood and the purpose for which it was intended, in those parts there were few large trees, but acres, or even miles, of thick coppice with paths arched over in summer like green tunnels. One thing we liked to do was to follow these paths, so we came to know the woods very well. In other parts there were tall oaks, chestnuts and beeches rising above the lower woodland, or a clump of pine trees, or dark, sombre yews or hollies. In such places there were red squirrels, now become so rare after the ravages of the grey 'tree rat' which came from Canada, a creature that does incalculable harm to the trees and has none of the charm of the lovely, little red squirrel. It was one of my ambitions to rear a young squirrel that would go about with me, but although I reared many young birds and rabbits I never achieved this.

In one spot beside the marsh of which I have written there were many fine beech trees; this was a specially good place for squirrels. Among these trees were tall pyramids of poles often built round a tree-trunk for seasoning and looking like wigwams. We found a way into one of these wigwams, and we turned it into a house. We lined the floor with dried sphagnum moss, rushes and marsh mint for the smell, so that it was dry and warm even in wet weather. We called it 'The Skew', which came about by an odd confusion. For the sake of secrecy we decided to refer to it by the first two letters of 'Squirrel's Nest', but instead of saying S. N. we said S. Q. and the name stuck. We had a fire outside on which we boiled a kettle, fried potatoes, cooked small trout or moorhens' eggs, or stewed apples with blackberries picked near by. We were very free. We would go off, in summer, with some food in our pockets in the morning and be seen no more until teatime. Often on wet days we stayed in our little house warm and comfortable, eating our food and reading while the rain poured down outside.

Occasionally I would go off with one of the village boys fishing or bird-nesting or on some jaunt. I remember one evening when one of them asked if I would like to come with him to catch efts. It was down at the bottom of the hill, where the stream ran under the road. He had some sticks, with lengths of line and bent pins for hooks, and he said the efts would bite on the worms which he carried in a tin so we could pull them out of the pond where they were to be found.

We went by the lane that ran below the wooded hill to the Hole, a hollow place where four lanes crossed. The one on the left climbed a steep hill by the wood, that on the right climbed another hill. We took the one that went straight on. About a quarter of a mile past the crossroads we climbed over a gate into a meadow. Across the meadow was a group of farm buildings, made of timbers tarred black, and roofed with tiles weathered and faded to a warm, rosy red, with patches of green moss and gold and grey lichens. These black-timbered barns and cow-sheds were common in that district and many years' exposure to the soft, damp air had weathered them into warm, mellow colours. In front of the buildings was the pond where we were to look for efts.

It was one of those golden summer evenings after a hot day, the air warm and still, the sun getting low in the west. The meadow stretched away, a brilliant green made golden by the evening light, cropped short by grazing cattle except round the pond where it was lush and green. The pond was fringed with clumps of blue-green reeds with little bronze flowers. There were patches of bright yellow kingcups in the water, with marsh mint and forget-me-nots and small white stars of crow-foot.

At one end of the pond was a kind of sloping beach where cows and horses came to drink and splash. Here the ground was poached by their feet, but the rest of the pond was surrounded by miniature cliffs capped with short grass. Where the evening sun shone on the banks they were a brilliant reddish yellow, and in the shadowed parts a cool, mauvish colour. There were a great many swallows which nested in the farm buildings, and they flew low over the meadow, suddenly shooting up into the air and then down again to skim across the surface of the pond, just dipping into the water here and there to make a silver splash.

I do not remember if we caught many efts, but I do remember them looking rather like lizards, some with crests and frills on their backs; and I remember it as one of those enchanted summer evenings, warm and scented with the honey-sweet smell of little mauve thistles; I remember how the gnats hung and danced over the water in trails and clouds shot through with golden light; how blue the forget-me-nots were in the water and how gold their centres were; and how the marsh mint smelt where we crushed it.

Water

I FIND I have a tendency to remember things in groups of a kind: for instance, water, sounds, smells, people. I have written already of water in describing the well, the pump and the springs. But water, in the forms of small lakes, ponds and streams, played a large part in my life.

At the bottom of the hill, down below our cottage, was a place where two streams joined. One came, as far as my knowledge of it went, across meadowland where the short turf was undercut into little yellow, green-capped cliffs by the meandering of the stream. The other flowed along the bottom of the valley below the forest-covered hill. The first passed under the road, where it was crossed by a small bridge, to join the second stream on the far side. The two together then formed a larger stream, which continued right into the woodland. On the one side, the left bank going downstream, the trees came down to the water's edge with grassy banks and clearings; but on the other the woods were separated from the stream by a stretch of marshy land. I was told that years before the marsh had been clear water but had gradually silted up, compressing the stream into its narrow channel. The marsh was full of rushes, marsh mint and kingcups and many flowers which loved the damp, such as irises and forget-me-nots with, in the drier parts, ragged robin and campion and pink centaury, or tea-flower, as we called it, for it was said that the old people made a medicinal tea of it. It was a great place for frogs; in hot, sultry weather I have known

the still, thick air to vibrate with their croaking; and many
moorhens nested there.

This stretch of the stream was, I should say, about half a
mile long. It was no longer just a brook but had become a small
river, running smoothly for most of its way, with an occasional
sparkle over a shallow, shaly stretch followed by deep,
dark pools reflecting the sombre green of the trees; or sometimes peaty brown with blue and purple ripples where the
sky was reflected. I have spent many a summer evening
here fishing, many a day wandering by the stream when it was
in full spate after winter rains, or in the early spring, when
the pale sunlight through the bare branches and the blue
sparkle on the water where it reflected the spring sky seemed
a counterpart to the note of the first chiff-chaff. On still,
warm summer evenings I have crept along the bank, tense with
excitement as I carried my rod in my hand. There would be
no sound but the murmur of the water, the thin song of the
gnats as they danced above the pools in mazy hypnotic skeins,
or the sudden plop! and the widening rings where a trout had
risen to a fly. Can there have been anything quite like this! To
see the shadowy forms of trout sliding under the banks; to cast
one's line and feel the sudden tension as the trout took the bait,
then the trembling wriggle of line and rod; and then to see the
trout swinging madly in the air as one's hand travelled down the
wet line to grasp the slippery, jumping fish. It was not very
superior fishing; my rod was a hazel stick cut from the woods,
with staples for runners and a cotton reel with a nail in the side
to wind it in. The trout were only little brook trout and my bait
was a worm, but there was never such fishing as this! How often
have I come home tired, dirty, probably wet and eaten by
mosquitoes; but with half a dozen fine, small trout on a hazel
wand. Sometimes I would set night lines from a peg in the bank
on which I caught trout or maybe eels – long, slithering things
which wound the line into a terrible tangle if they were not
settled quickly.

And then the evenings by those pools, growing deeper as the
dusk fell. As I crouched on the bank, I would see a water vole
come out of his hole on the opposite side. I stayed so still that
he did not see me; and there he would sit washing his face

with his paws, his bright little eyes twinkling like stars; the air
was so still that I could hear him crunching the cresses across
the water. If I made a movement he would take to the water,
and swim off with his back just showing and a long arrowy
ripple spreading away from his nose. And then there were the
smells: of the water; of the marsh mint where I had crushed it;
of the muddy banks; of the worms in my tin; and the smell of
the fish on my hands.

As well as the smells there was the quiet; not a dead but a
living silence, full of small noises and stirrings of life. These
ranged from the last song of a late singing thrush to the
'Coorock!' of a moorhen, the booming of a bumble-dor or
the small squeak of a bat; and at length it was so still that a
white ghost moth hovering in the dusk was almost a noise. And
behind it all I was aware of the countryside stretching away on
every hand, across the fields to the farms and cottages where
lamps were beginning to shine; or deep into the woods where
night creatures, foxes and badgers, night hawks and owls were
moving. The slow white mist came creeping across the marsh
and the low-lying meadows until the trees were dark blots
against the evening sky, their feet lost in a nebulous sea.

At the end of the marshy stretch the stream broadened out
into a pool in front of the ruined watermill. A rough road led to
the mill, with a brick wall beside the water on which one could
sit to fish. Some water escaped down the disused shute, where
the great wheel was still in its place – it was a strange, damp,
dripping place half-hidden by bushes and rank growth, the
timbers rotted and full of holes and the mill wheel making
creaking noises and hollow splashes as the water fell on the
slimy brickwork. The mill seemed haunted by its past activity.
When I clambered about inside among the rusting machinery
and the rotting sacks and ropes, the smell of flour and meal
seemed to hang about in the shadowy stairways and dusty
rooms, and among the cobwebby rafters. The broken shutter of
a window moved in the wind, a door or hatchway creaked, and
birds and rats made scurrying, rustling noises. It had not been
used for many years; but for some time a solitary man, known as
the Brownie, lived there, though heaven knows on what he
lived. He was seldom seen; but one evening I heard the strokes

of an axe and, creeping up to peer down into the hollow below
the mill from behind a tree trunk, I saw him cutting wood. My
memory is of a dark black and brown man of a kind which was
common in Sussex in those days. His skin was a dark all-over
brownish or clay colour with no red in it; his hair, I remember
he wore no hat, a dark brown or black, worn very short; his
clothes were dusty greys, browns and bleached colours —
probably corduroy trousers, a faded shirt with no collar and a
bleached brown waistcoat. I believe he was eventually had up
for sheep stealing and carried off by 'Authority'. I wonder if
they locked him up in the 'loony bin', or put him in an institu-
tion and made him clean and respectable, till he died like a
caged animal, or like poor John Clare.

After the mill the stream entirely altered in character. It
became a clear stream rushing among stones and boulders,
winding in and out between small hills covered with trees and
hazel coverts. In summer the whole place was full of broom,
campions, ragged robin and banks of foxgloves; and, earlier,
primroses grew in profusion among the hazels, with their crinkled leaves and pale masses of flowers against the brown of the
woods and last year's leaves; and before the primroses came
wind-flowers like drifts of late snow. In sheltered spots behind
boulders the violets flourished, while down by the stream or on
a sunny bank the celandines shone as though they were
enamelled among their glossy spade-shaped leaves. How many
spring nosegays have I picked of purple-blue violets, gold
celandines and white wind-flowers? The ground was covered
with a thick layer of leaf mould into which you could burrow
with your hands, down to the yellow clay and shaly rock. It was
the haunt of many birds and small wild animals. In spring the
air rang with the songs of willow-wrens, white-throats, chiff-
chaffs, thrushes, blackbirds, dunnocks, small darting wrens
with shrill voices, and over all was the calling of the cuckoo.
Scores of rabbits bred in the sides of the little hills. In the
remoter parts were foxes, badgers, stoats and weasels.

A common sound was the cry of a rabbit being hunted by a
stoat or a weasel, and I have often come upon a newly killed
rabbit with the tell-tale marks at the back of its ears. When the
doe has a litter she will go off foraging and drag loose earth

round the mouth of her burrow to hide it. I used to pull the earth away with my hands and then, with a long stick with a fork at the end, I would thrust my arm down the tunnel, give the stick a twist and bring up the bedding with the young rabbits. I learnt to do this from one of my friends who was often in the woods with his gun and his dog. If they were big enough I would sometimes take them home and rear them on milk with a teaspoon. For a while they would be quite tame, but they usually became wilder as they grew and eventually returned to their natural life. I often noticed that the colour of the young rabbits appeared to vary with the locality and soil in which they lived; most, in the deeper part of the woods being dark greyish brown, while others in exposed sandy banks were paler, the colour of the Belgian hare; but the pale ones would become darker on exposure to the light. It was by no means uncommon to see a black or a white rabbit among the wild ones. I have heard that this is caused by an 'escape' breeding with them; but I have wondered whether a white one may be an albino, like a white blackbird, or the black ones a kind of 'sport'. There were also numbers of adders which one would come upon coiled up in a sunny patch on a path or a bank; but although I was bare legged and wearing sandals I never felt any apprehension, and I do not remember hearing of people being bitten.

Among the banks of brambles, alders and hazels, and in thick patches of wild rose were many birds' nests. The wonderfully snug nests of chaffinches can usually be found in a thick hawthorn bush, blackbirds and thrushes build mostly in hedges or clumps of bushes, the missel-thrush or 'storm cock' in the fork of a branch where it springs from a tree, often high up. Robins seem to like a hole in a wall or any sheltered place, they will often build in a flower pot or even an old saucepan or kettle if it is in a safe place. Jenny-wrens will build in a faggot pile or among any dense, thick cover or in a convenient hole. One day a little bird flew out from a thick tussocky patch among small bushes, and there I found the nest of a willow-wren – such a neat little nest and so many tiny, pinkish-splotched eggs for such a small bird! On a spring morning the air rang with the songs of these enchanting little birds – to me one of the sweetest of all songs. Woodlarks sang with their ecstatic trills as they parachuted from a high branch, the very spirit of a spring morning; wrens shrilled from thickets, and dunnocks, those gentle, creeping, sweet-natured birds with their mauvish brown and chestnut plumage, sang their blameless jingling songs. Down by the water the pied wagtails – sallys or dish-washers as we called them – bobbed and wagged on the stones, crying 'Chizzick! Chizzick!', and whitethroats flitted from spray to spray, their song cascading from them in a tumbling rush with odd, harsh notes adding a piquant sharpness.

I constantly haunted this stream so that it became a kind of obsession with me; and indeed it has remained so all my life. I have seen many beautiful streams and rivers since then, but I doubt if any one of them has played so large a part in my life or left such an indelible impression. I have one memory which may seem strange: in fact more than once when I have mentioned it people have obviously thought it a little odd, or perhaps that I was telling them something of a tale, but it is perfectly true and seemed to me quite natural. When I had been a long while there by myself with the sound of the water in my ears I fancied that I heard voices, even a sudden small shout or a burst of laughter so that I looked up to see who was there, but there was no one. I believe there is a perfectly natural explanation of this. If one is alone with the constant sound of water it sets up vibrations – I do not know what to call them – so that one can imagine that one hears voices. It may be that it occurs only to some people – as only some people (myself included) can find water with a hazel fork. I only know that it has happened to me many times.

The stream ran in loops and bends, sometimes quite deep and dark under an overhanging bank; then rushing among boulders; then in a wide sparkling stickle. Here and there were considerable pools, big and deep enough for a swim. After a rough, stony passage the water suddenly became calm and still on the surface, the colour of old ale with flecks of foam. The force of the stream, especially when great quantities of water came down after heavy rain, carved out hollow places beneath overhanging banks of yellow clay and greyish shale. On the one side the water was deep beneath the bank; on the other was a gravelly beach. The water was as cold as ice in the hottest weather; so cold was it that I would put my foot in and take it out again until I became accustomed to it, like getting into a hot bath. There is a peculiar kind of pleasure to be had from lying or squatting submerged in a pool among foaming or still brown water, with nothing visible but one's head and the sun hot on one's face. In such a position one appears to be nearly invisible. I have had a kingfisher perch quite near to me or a dipper bowing on a stone a few feet from my face. All around one sees the woods, the grassy banks and the flowers with a sensation of strangeness, as though one had become absorbed into nature. This sense of being part of nature is continued by lying on the hot, sun-baked shale of the beach, experiencing a double sensation compounded of the icy tingle of the water and the hot power of the sun.

We were very free. In summer, like a ritual, we were given a bathing dress and a pair of sandals and we would be off for whole days, scrambling among the little hills and rocks, bathing in the pools or paddling in the shallows, sailing small, home-made boats down the swift stream, steering them with long hazel rods over the quiet pools or shooting the rapids. I have made many small boats out of a piece of flat wood sharpened at one end to a prow, with a mast made from a stick jammed into a hole, and a sail made of paper or a piece of material; and very good sailers they were in a following wind. We would eat our lunch squatting on a boulder or lying in the sun beside the water.

It was in the little brown streams that I caught my trout, mostly in the pools between the reaches of broken water. In such pools one could watch them. Trout often have a regular route in such pools, especially when they are shut up in them in dry weather. From behind a bush I would watch them, and if I saw a fine one I would study him before trying to catch him. When he had made his round I waited for him to appear, coming towards me, marking the place where he was likely to turn; as he turned, swimming away from me, I gently dropped my hook baited with a worm behind him. It had to be done quietly so that I did not frighten him away. He continued to the far end of the pool, turned, and came towards me again. When he saw the worm he would stop, then suddenly make a rush and take it. I then had to strike to make sure of him. There was one pool with steep banks that held a number of fine fish, but because of the nature of the banks I could never reach it without a stone or a branch falling into the water and frightening the fish. One never-to-be-forgotten evening I managed to get within casting distance without making any noise, and there I crouched watching my chance. There was one splendid trout that I longed to catch. I held my breath as he went on his round, and as he passed me and turned away I dropped my baited hook with all the skill and care I could manage. I waited, hardly daring to breathe. Round he came, swimming towards me; he turned, stopped and then rushed at the worm. I was so excited that I struck too soon, but he was just hooked enough. I also struck too hard, so that he flew out of the water in an arc. The gut cast broke, but he landed on the little beach in front of me. In a moment he would have been back in the water, but I pounced on him and managed to hold him though he flapped and wriggled and was as slippery as ice. I had him! A sharp tap on the back of his head on a stone and there he was – the finest trout I think I ever caught in that brook, a full half-pound in weight.

In the estate there was a fine pond, or small lake, where I caught many perch. It was rumoured that there were tremendous carp in this pool, 'as big as a man's leg', and pike as well. Often on a still evening I have heard a tremendous splash and seen great rings of water spreading away across the lake and breaking in small waves against the banks. I longed to hook one of these fabulous monsters, but they were too cunning for me, though I did bring back many a string of small perch.

It was a fine piece of water for swimming. I used to go there before breakfast on summer mornings and come back feeling at peace with the world, with that peculiar sense of physical well-being that can, I suppose, be experienced by no one in such perfection as by a small, happy boy. I remember wonderful summer mornings when I went there with my brother before he went off to the First World War. Strong swimmer that he was, he would swim right across the lake, but I sported in the shallows. It was the home of many ducks, coots, moorhens and other water creatures. One of the loveliest things

I ever saw, and of which I never tired, was a flight of duck appearing high in the air then descending upon the pool in a series of wide spiral sweeps growing smaller in circumference, until they ended in a long glide, landing with a swish and a silver gleam on the glassy surface. I know nothing which, for pure beauty of rhythm and pattern, surpasses a flight of duck against a pale-gold evening sky, with a pool below, bright gleaming silver in the light and deep purple-browns and greens below the sombre shade of great trees.

One evening I shall never forget for sheer magic. It had been a hot golden September day. I had been fishing with my back to a cornfield where the corn was in stooks ready for carting, the strange shapes of the stooks in rhythmic lines on the rising surface of the stubble field – the very rhythm of harvest. I was engrossed in my fishing. After the heat of the day the dew began to fall, so that the grass at my feet was drenched with moisture. A perfect stillness lay over the countryside, a stillness so intense that a harvest mouse creaking a straw was a startling sound. As the purple dusk deepened I laid my rod on the bank and turned round. It is this moment that I can never forget and that I have tried to express in painting many times. Over the rounded stubble field and the strange shapes of the stooks in the purple haze of a September evening hung the most enormous golden moon I have ever seen. It was just above the horizon, tremendous, unearthly, almost frightening in its vastness. I stared at it with awe, half-delighted, half-afraid. It was the summation of all moonrises, possessing, with all its charm, an elemental force, a sense of things to be marvelled at but never understood.

This same part of the estate by the lake is associated with another indelible impression. The land sloped down from the road and the park wall to the level of the lake. One autumn morning I was there when they were ploughing up the stubble. In those days the ploughing tended to be a little longer after harvest than it is now and, at a guess, I should say it was an October morning. But it was a fresh day with a breeze, and a blue and white sky, and sun and shadow. As I stood by the park wall looking down towards the lake, I saw a sight that can only be imagined by young people today. The ploughing was done with teams of horses as this was long before the days of tractors, and that morning I saw not one but a number of teams all ploughing at once. I do not know how many there were but I stood entranced, small boy as I was, by the coming and going of those splendid teams. As one was going away from me down the slope of the field, another might be coming towards me, the horses plodding up the slope to turn at the headland for the downward journey. The movement of the horses, their action, the nodding of their heads and their manes blowing in the breeze was as fine a sight as one might see; and when they reached the headland the skill with which the ploughman handled the plough and controlled the horses, the strange mixture of clumsiness, strength and beauty, was something that no one who has not seen it can imagine. As there was no noise, as there is with a tractor, one could hear as well as see, so that the plod of the horses' feet, the jingle of the harness, the ploughman's voice as he spoke to them and encouraged them, and the special hissing noise as the ploughshare went into the ground and the mould board turned over the beautiful brown furrow, all added up to something complete. If you add the freshness of the air, the smell of the newly turned earth, the sun and shadow chasing each other across the landscape, and the crying of gulls and rooks as they followed the plough, it completed a kind of perfection. I cannot help thinking in Biblical language, in the language of the great Authorized Version: 'Man goeth forth unto his work and to his labour until the evening.' 'Whatsoever a man soweth, that shall he also reap.' 'Except a corn of wheat fall into the ground and die, it abideth alone . . .' There was a rhythm in life then which was like the rhythm of the scriptures.

Where the stream in the woods went to I do not know. I suppose I could refer to a map and find out. But I am writing of things as they seemed to me then, a small boy whose whole world lay within a radius of five miles or so. It must be remembered that in those days, if one lived as we did with our journeys limited to the range of walking, of a pony trap, or of cycling, one lived in a small, contained world. One's life was in a sense, more intense than it is now when people think nothing of a journey of fifty miles. The world of those few lanes, meadows and streams, of the shop, the Post Office and the church, was the only world that mattered to me. I was in a state of innocence; and I should like to convey that state if I can. The little stream left our world when it passed under a bridge made of timbers and covered with earth; it disappeared into further woods and so out of our lives.

It may appear that in some of my remarks I am anticipating what I came to feel later, or crediting myself with a more precise definition of thought than I was capable of having at that time, for I was only a small boy. But although I would not claim that I could have put my ideas into words, as I can now, I do believe that I had vague apprehensions of ideas that have since become important to me. The incident of the sinister aeroplane, for example, is not exaggerated. I felt it as I have described it. So I will venture to describe events or ideas that occurred to me, that, however vague they were at the time, were nevertheless positive, if embryonic.

One such event occurred on an evening in May, a fair, settled evening with a wonderful clarity of light; one of those evenings in which a blessing seems to lie upon the earth. I was alone. I stood upon the little bridge by the mill looking across the marshy land and the river. I remember it for the number of cuckoos calling to each other across the woods, that dearest sound of spring. And I remember it too because it is the first time that I can recall having a strong impulse to express myself in terms of painting, and particularly because I had no impulse to paint a purely realistic picture of the scene; but an impulse, in some way that I apprehended only dimly, to express in visual terms the emotion that I felt, as a musician might in terms of music. It stands out in my mind as being the first time that such an impulse occurred to me. I suppose I was about twelve years old.

A short distance below our cottage there was a stile in the hedge, from which a path led across the meadows. After crossing two or three fields it climbed a fairly steep hill to another stile, which led into a wood. At the top of this hill, right up against the wood, there was a place where I liked to sit and I have often stayed there for some time sitting on the grass, looking down at the valley and the part of the village where our cottage was. This was really a small hamlet a mile or more from the village proper. From where I sat I had a bird's eye view of the cottages, including ours; of the shop, with the stables and barns belonging to it; of the hill above and the lane which twisted and turned and finally plunged steeply down into the valley. I could see all that I knew, every field and hedgerow, the cottage gardens, the people going about their business; and it seemed to me as though I could not only see but identify myself with that little world where I belonged. I cannot describe the intense pleasure that this gave me. If it appears that I am exaggerating the emotion that I felt then, I can quote Thomas Traherne writing of how he felt as a small boy: 'The green trees when I saw them first through one of the gates transported and ravished me, their sweetness and unusual beauty made my heart to leap, and almost mad with ecstasy, they were such strange and wonderful things'; and John Constable, 'The scenes of my childhood made me a painter.' I am in good company.

But one special feeling came to me, sitting at that spot and brooding on what I saw. It has stayed with me for the rest of my life. I can describe it briefly as my first discovery of the true nature of the English countryside.

There are, in a sense, two different kinds of nature, savage nature 'red in tooth and claw', and nature dominated by and in turn affecting the life of man – in other words domestic or rural nature.

England is, in essence, a small, ordered land. It gained its ordered character largely in the eighteenth century, when so much attention was given to farming and so many estates were planned; and this planning created the small, intimate, ordered beauty which we have come to regard as essentially English. From this time, and from our heritage of Elizabethan and Jacobean houses and cottages, has come a countryside which is a curious, and curiously natural, blending of the formal and the informal, of the natural and the stylized. It has created a country of estates, farms and villages, each with its manor house, its farmhouses, cottages, orchards and gardens. The very woods and copses are not wild in the primeval sense of the word; the very brooks and rivers are part of a man-created landscape.

If one stands upon a hill overlooking a stretch of rural England at its best, one cannot but feel that there is not a single foot of ground, not a hill, wood or meadow, not a field, path or hedge-enclosed lane, not a brook or river, no stretch of cornfield or sheep-sprinkled downland which is not associated with human life. The lowing of the cattle, the barking of the farm dogs, the sound of bells from the ancient church, the chiming of the clock, the songs of the birds in the trees and hedges, the bright flowers in the banks, are not just nature. They are the expression of a way of life, a kind of rural continuity. It is this nature, rather than savage nature, which has inspired our poets, our novelists, our painters.

W. H. Hudson has written of this sense of human life in nature in *Afoot in England*.

I am struck with the thought that the sweet sensations produced in me by the scene differ in character from the feeling I have had in other solitary places. The peculiar sense of satisfaction, of restfulness, of peace, experienced here is very perfect; but in the wilderness where man has never been, or at all events left no trace of his former presence, there is ever a mysterious sense of loneliness, of desolation, underlying our pleasure in nature. – This, I take it, is a satisfaction, a sweetness and peace to the soul, because it carries with it a sense of the continuity of the human race, its undying vigour, its everlastingness.

The sun and the moon rise and set. The seasons come and go, spring, summer, autumn, winter. But the very seasons of the year are connected with human life – spring, summer, autumn, winter: birth, childhood, manhood, old age, death, and burial in an ancient churchyard with the cawing of rooks in the elms and the sounds from the neighbouring farmyard. Everything adds up to a fullness and completeness. In the spring children gather buttercups and daisies and put them in jam-jars in cottage windows. As the seasons change so the cycle of the church moves on: the snow and the cold; the yellow light streaming from the church door and the sound of Christmas carols; the sharp, cold air of spring, the lengthening days; Good Friday and Easter Day, and the Easter hymns and birds' eggs like bits of blue sky in the hedges and bright-coloured Easter eggs on the breakfast table with the Lenten season over; the fullness of summer; the mellow ripeness of autumn, Harvest Festival; 'The valleys also shall stand so thick with corn, that they shall laugh and sing.'

Now 'the winter storms begin', and soon it is Christmas again. Some have been born, some have passed on, and so it continues: the year of the seasons, the year of the church, the year of human life. This, with its underlying sense of Divine Purpose, of harmony between nature and human life, of man living not against but with the great rhythms of nature is not just something pleasant and romantic. It is an essential of human life without which comes spiritual poverty.

I do not claim that I, as a small boy, sat upon the hillside looking down upon the village, felt all this as I have written it now, or that I could have put it into words. But I do claim, and the memory is so clear and sharp that I feel justified in claiming it, that I felt stirrings, an awakening consciousness of something which has grown in strength as I have matured, until it has become the very basis of my life and my work as a painter.

Haymaking

LOOKING back in reminiscent mood, I am conscious of what a number of small everyday events there were in our lives, which to us were natural but which, by the passage of time and the changes which have come about in the character and pace of daily life, have assumed a kind of intensity. No doubt the passing of the years and the coloured mists of time have given these daily commonplaces something which was not so obvious at the time; or so some people would say. But I find it hard to believe that things which have left such an indelible impression, not only on me but on others, can be only a matter of emotional distortion. I believe that something good and simple has gone out of daily life with their passing.

One of these annual festivals – for so they were – was the hay harvest. In trying to recall such an event I will condense many occasions into one, taking the liberty of writing as though all were perfect.

It is one of those perfect June mornings when the sun rises through a golden haze and the hedgerow elms stand like dark phantoms against the pearly sky, their feet lost in trails of dense, white mist. The grass is heavy with a drenching dew and, as the sun rises, the sky becomes an intense gold, and a golden light shines through the feathery masses of hay grass drooping with the burden of silver drops. As the heat increases and the white mist begins to disperse I hear the whirring of the hay-cutter, drawn by two horses, the farmer sitting on a sprung seat at the back. First I see him dimly on the far side of the meadow, the lower half of the horses and the machine hidden by the tall grass, but then he reaches the corner of the field, where he turns and approaches in the shadow of the hedge, the nodding heads of the horses coming nearer and the steam of their breath just visible in the damp air. They reach the second corner of the meadow so that I can see the clumsy–skilful handling of the man as he turns them, and hear his voice in a chant, 'Way, woa – woa! Way – woa!' Now they are coming towards me on the nearside of the meadow, the grass falling in a swathe as they pass, leaving the pale green of the under-stalks, that peculiar green of a newly cleared meadow. On they go into the distance, and so round the meadow in decreasing sweeps until only the grass in the centre is standing, a straight wall of dark green crowned with the swaying tops of the grasses and flowers in an old-fashioned mixed meadow. Often at this stage one or two men and boys with guns, dogs and sticks will arrive, for there may be rabbits, hares or partridges in this last piece, which will bolt for the hedge as the grass falls.

Now the grass is cut and there it lies in heavy grey-green swathes with pale lines of the under-grass between until it is ready to turn.

When it is sufficiently dry what amounts to a rural festival begins. The meadow becomes a lively scene with men and boys, women, girls and children of all ages turning out for a strenuous holiday. The men wear trousers hitched up under their knees with straps or bands of straw, flannel shirts with no collars and the sleeves rolled up to show knotty, weathered arms; the boys are dressed in a similar way but quite often with knee breeches. All wear some kind of hat, often round, wide-brimmed straw hats, yellow and stained with age and weather. One would not expect to see a man stripped to the waist as is common now, and they are probably wearing boots which, however clumsy they may appear to be today, are best for heavy work and rough ground. The women and girls wear cotton dresses and a variety of hats, sunbonnets being by no means uncommon. The children are like miniatures of their elders.

In this job of turning the swathes the women are as useful and as skilful as the men. They use two-pronged forks or long-handled wooden hay rakes which have a wide sweep, the rake

itself with its wooden teeth being sometimes straight and sometimes slightly curved, with struts from the handle to the bar of
the rake to strengthen it. These rakes are light and strong
enabling one to turn considerable masses of hay without them
catching in the grass as a metal garden rake would. By contact
with many hands they are often worn and polished quite
smooth. Round and round the field the haymakers go with a
rather crab-like sideways walk, each turning a swathe with a
skilful flick and twist of the arms. Often they work in a stag-
gered formation so that each is following another further into
the field, and not straight behind. In this way no grass is left
unturned. As the sun and the breeze dry the grass it turns a
greyer colour and becomes lighter in texture, so that it is raised
above the meadow instead of lying flat as it did when it was first
cut.

It is a very gay, happy scene. The weathered figures of the
men and boys with their duller colours act as a foil to the gay
blues, whites and pinks of the women and girls. The whole
meadow is full of chatter, back-chat and laughter as those with
the rakes go round and round the meadow, following the first
movement of the horses and the cutter. In and out among the
workers the smaller children run and tumble and roll over and
over in the hay. When there is a break for refreshment they all
gather together and sit, lie and sprawl on the now drying hay,
rather like Pieter Brueghel's picture, *The Hay Harvest*, chattering and laughing like a flock of guinea-fowl as they eat their food
and drink cold tea or cider.

The length of this operation, 'haymaking' in the full meaning
of the word, depends upon the weather. The sooner hay is
'made' and the less it is drenched with rain or dried up with sun
the better it will be. Then it is raked up and built into haycocks
by men with two-tined hayforks to be ready for carting.

The right time to load it into the wagons is a matter of
judgment that calls for considerable skill and experience on the
part of the farmer. I believe it is a kind of instinct which is only
acquired after years of practice. If it is too dry and overmade it
will lose its nature; if it is too green and moist it may overheat in
the stack and spoil or even catch fire. It is quite extraordinary
how hot a stack can become in the middle if it does overheat. I

have sat against a newly built stack on the leeward side, and I
have felt it become so hot as to be unpleasant.

Finally, it may be after several days or according to the
weather, comes the carting. This is a splendid sight as great
wagons, or wains, drawn by heavy horses rumble into the fields,
being guided with remarkable skill by the carters. I doubt if
anyone who has not tried it or seen it done can appreciate the
skill which is required to bring a wagon and horses through a
gateway. When the wagons arrive the loading begins. Nowadays one is accustomed to seeing the hay being baled on the
meadow and then loaded on to a trailer dragged by a tractor.
But this was a far more complex business. To the casual specta-
tor it may have appeared to be the mere piling of hay into a
wagon. In fact it required a unison of action, an actual rhythm
which, if broken, could hamper the whole. A man, or a respon-
sible lad, led the horses, and he had to judge the distance, which
must be neither too far nor not far enough. Before each forward
movement he would shout 'Hold tight!', which was the signal
for the men on the wagon to lean on their hayforks and sway to
the jolting. On each side of the wagon men would load the hay,
this operation being also a matter of great skill. If one watched
an experienced man he would gather up just the right quantity
of hay and swing it up to the men on the wagon with a
minimum of effort. But one had only to watch an inexperienced
man to see that the ease was apparent. He would probably
gather too little, or too much, and lose half of it or deliver it in so
awkward a manner as to break the rhythm of loading.

When the wagon is full it may be led to the stackyard by the
farm, or often a stack is built in the corner of the meadow. The
building of the stack calls for as much skill and experience as
any other part of haymaking. I have often watched the way in
which the men receive the hay from a loader and pack it so that
the whole mass is distributed and built until it is firm and solid,
the sides of the stack neither bulging nor receding. A well-built
stack is as firm and solid as a house, and when it is finally
thatched it will stand against all wind and weather until it is
needed. There must be many people today who have never seen
a haystack built, or indeed seen one at all, for they have been
replaced by piles of bales covered with a sheet.

One more part of this great ceremony, for such it was, is the clearing of the meadow with a horse-rake, a wide two-wheeled affair. The rake at the back consists of curved prongs fixed to a bar and operated by the driver. With his left hand he holds the reins and with his right he raises or lowers the rake by a lever. He travels across the field, and the art, which I know from experience to be far from easy, lies in raising the rake at the right moment so the raked-up hay lies in straight lines across the meadow. When this is complete it is once more gathered into haycocks and carried to the stack.

The final act of this rural festival comes when the horse is unhitched and the horse-rake is backed up against the hedge, the hand rakes and forks are piled into the wagon, the children climb in for the homeward ride, and finally all that gay, chattering throng streams through the gateway into the lane to wander home, tired and happy, between hedges and banks damp with dew and smelling of new-made hay and honeysuckle. The great full moon, gold, mild and settled, sails up from behind dark masses of woodland. Nightjars begin to swoop and skirl in the trees and the lamps begin to shine in the cottage windows. The gate is pulled to and latched and, after all the days of hot sunshine, chatter and work and all the happiness and activity, as the last stragglers disappear towards the village, the silent meadow lies glimmering and pale in the owl-light, empty and damp with falling dew and filling the quiet air with fragrance.

Wild Flowers

AMONG the greatest of the treasures which I remember is the old-fashioned hayfield. I have already written of haymaking but as much pleasure was to be found in the meadow in May and June before the time of cutting. At the back of our cottage was a meadow which was up for hay most years, I had only to cross a stile to be in it, which, of course, I knew I must never do while the grass was growing. But what a growth that was!

First there came the flush of young grass in April, when the warmer weather and the showers started everything on its spring course. The grass grew higher until it was a swaying mass of every imaginable kind of grass – some feathery; some strong, straight and purplish green; the rye grass with its sharp zig-zag looking heads; cock's foot and timothy and fescue; fine-bladed grass and broad-bladed grass, with every variety of green, grey-green and silver-green and a faint haze of golden and pinkish green; some a rosy colour, some bronze, some purple. On an early summer morning when the dew was heavy the feathery heads would be suffused with gold from the rising sun; in wet weather the whole sparkled with silver drops, and when there was a breeze the grasses swayed with a movement like water.

As the season advanced so came the flowers, and what a company they were! Purple vetches with branching arms and frail tendrils clambered among the stronger grasses. Pink and white clover filled the air with scent. Yarrow, bed-straw and crane's-bill were mixed with buttercups and reddish sorrel.

There were rose-red campions and ragged robin, yellow rattle and purple bugle and sheets of white moon-daisies. There were hawkbit and tansy, little reddish and purple thistles, sow thistles and splendid yellow dandelions which turned to silver clocks. Round the outside of the meadow were silver-white banks of cow-parsley, or ladies' laces, low down were the aromatic ground ivy, little creeping buttercups, eggs and bacon, and among the white daisies the frail lilac flowers of the ladies' smocks. There were ox-eye daisies and camomile and mallows, and every shade of pink, white, gold and blue that one could imagine.

On a fair summer morning, with larks filling the air with song and a gentle breeze moving the grasses, there was no more beautiful sight than such a meadow, and I am glad to have seen the white sheets of moon-daisies shining in the light of a full moon.

But the flowers grew not only in the meadows. It seemed as though every bank and hedgerow blossomed like a flower garden. Beside the road there were little copses and hollows where, among the slender trunks of young trees, the grass was brilliant green and spangled over with the gold of celandines, the purple of violets, the delicate lilac of the ladies' smocks and all manner of little creeping plants and flowers, brilliant and shining in the spring sunshine. In shadier and damper parts were strange, rather sinister, but beautiful plants – the purple and gold of nightshade, freaked and spotted orchids, white orchids, looking rather ghostly in damp, boggy patches and the incredible blue of forget-me-nots. The short grass on the banks was sprinkled with white daisies, the buds quite pink as they unfolded. In the woods were small patches of land which had been cultivated and were now neglected. Here grew carpets of wild strawberry with white flowers in spring, scarlet pimpernels and masses of little, bright, wild pansies and toad-flax. In damp places by streams and ponds were kingcups, shining gold against the water, which was spangled over the white stars of water crowfoot.

It was not only the banks and the meadows that blossomed, but also the hedges. In the early spring came the frail white flowers of the blackthorn at the time of the cold biting winds

– the blackthorn winter. Later came the hawthorn, richer and heavier than the blackthorn, filling the air with pungent scent; and then the flat, creamy-coloured plates of the elderflower. With the blossom came the leaves, the tiny crinkled leaves of the hawthorn which were nearly as vivid as the flowers; the children called them bread and cheese and ate them on the way to school. The beech leaves and the leaves of the lime trees were soft and almost transparent, looking like green flames when the sun shone through them from behind, and they were seen against the darkness of hills which had a blue bloom on them like a ripe plum. The willows were little silver-green points as they burst from their buds, and the pussy willow was pure silver.

To see beech woods at one of their most perfect moments one must see them on a bright spring morning when the wood-wren is in full song. Gilbert White has written of this little bird, which is very similar to the chiff-chaff and the willow-wren, in *The Natural History of Selborne*. 'This last haunts only the tops of the trees in high beechen woods, and makes a sibilous grass-hopper like noise now and then, at short intervals, shaking a little with its wings when it sings.' I remember one of these little birds, which held me quite entranced as it flitted among the tender green leaves, illumined by the sun against a blue sky, some of the leaves being so pale in radiant light as to be almost white. The ecstatic trilling of the bird and his creeping, mouse-like movements, varied by the quivering of his wings as he flew from branch to branch, seemed the perfect equivalent of the sunshine and the mosaic of blue and silver as I looked upwards from where I sat against a tree root.

With full summer there were banks of wild roses particularly in one place down by the mill, where they grew in thousands so that one saw them from the little tight buds to the full open flower; and near the roses the honeysuckle hung in festoons. Later still the reverted fields in the woods were flaming masses of ragwort, St John's wort and enormous Scotch thistles with their regal crowns of purple flowers.

With the passing of the flowers came the fruits: blackberries and hips and haws, the flat blossoms of the elder changed to purple berries. The wayfaring tree had its clusters of purple-red berries, and the hazels were hung with clusters of nuts, first of all greenish yellow with a rosy bloom, until they ripened and turned brown. There were acorns in their neat cups, sweet chestnuts and conkers and beech nuts; and with the late sombre beech leaves went the 'Twite! Twite! Twite!' of the nuthatches, the perfect counterpart of this time as the song of the wood-wrens is in spring.

From spring onwards came the butterflies, brilliant yellow brimstones, every kind of white, tortoiseshell and red admiral and peacock in the gardens and the woodland rides; and in the meadows blue butterflies with a rosy sheen on them, and meadow browns, and orange-tips and tiny moths and the daylong churring of the grasshoppers, and at dusk the yellow-under-wing moths, the magpie moths and the white ghost-moths.

I do not write of these things as a naturalist or ornithologist. I am not even greatly concerned if I have got the names wrong, that is the proper names; as for the Latin names I never could master them. I write as much as I can in my seventies, as a small boy wandering in a state of innocence in an enchanted time when there was still a bloom on the world, among 'All Things Bright and Beautiful', and believing, with no shadow of doubt, that 'The Lord God made them all.'

Smells and Sounds

THE thought of marsh mint and sphagnum moss starts my mind running on smells and I become aware of how many there were and how large a part they played in my life. Nothing is more evocative than smell: the smell of mint with peas or new potatoes; the smell of the marsh mint down by the stream or in the shady woodland rides where the sun hardly seemed to penetrate; the smell of ground ivy with its little purple flower; the perfume of the lime trees in full bloom; the smell among the pines. The smell of apples, either kept apples in a loft in winter or fresh from the tree, is a fragrance that goes with the sharp taste and never travels. There was the smell of lavender, rosemary and southernwood in the gardens; of honeysuckle in the hedges; the heady smell of new-mown hay; the smell of sap where they had been stripping bark in the woods, and the peculiar smell of bracken, reminding one a little of bananas. The smell of wood smoke was common, for most of the cottages had wood fires and I associate it with tea in lonely spots, the water being boiled in large black kettles encrusted with wood smoke.

There is another smell which is peculiarly evocative, the smell of methylated spirits. It was common for ladies to have a silver kettle on a tray at the table, which was kept hot by a little spirit stove: my mother had such a stove. But for me it has a special connection. We used to go to tea at a cottage where a lady lived who was the daughter of a former Rector. I specially associate these tea-parties with Christmas, for we usually went into a room built on to the cottage for tea, where we ate scones with jam and cream and Christmas cake and pulled crackers. The kettle was boiled on a spirit stove and the whole place smelled of methylated spirits.

What a lot of smells there were: the sharp tang in the smell of a bunch of cowslips, the faint delicate smell of wild roses, the pungent, nutty smell of gorse flowering in hot sunshine.

There were special smells which went with the cottages: the smell of old-fashioned honeycombed bedspreads and feather beds; the smell of rain water in the bedroom jug; the smell of an old house that burns paraffin and wood. There was the old, old smell of the church; the smell of horse-chestnuts in bloom after a thunderstorm; and the pungent, musky smell of a fox deep in the woods. With the smells go the sounds. Our lives were very quiet, and since our senses were not dulled by the noise of cities we could be aware of small quiet sounds which many people never hear. Indeed I count myself fortunate in this as in so many ways, for sounds have always meant a great deal to me; they are, in their own way, as evocative as smells.

If I woke early in the morning the sounds varied according to the season. I liked to go to the window and lean out as the first faint streaks of light appeared. Over the horizon in the east was a faint golden light. On a fine summer morning a wonderful stillness brooded over the land and then, faint and far away, there came the crowing of a cock from a farmyard. A small, sleepy twittering came from the martins' nests under the eaves and, as the golden light grew brighter behind the dark mass of the woods, a ripple of song came from a robin in the faggot stack; and then, as though this was a signal, there followed such an outburst of song as can scarcely be imagined by those who have not heard it. The sudden flood of bird song on a perfect, early summer morning in a perfect setting of English country-side is one of the miracles granted to humans 'now in the time of this mortal life' – when every growing thing is drenched with dew and the air is drenched with golden light, and every cuckoo, lark, blackbird, thrush, robin, swallow, chaffinch, and every kind of songbird bursts forth in a cascade of jubilant sound.

For me sleep was impossible when this happened. I had to

rush out into that magical world, over the stile and across the meadows to the woods. The ground was soaking wet with dew, which rose in a grey mist as I brushed through the long grass and drenched my sandals and bare legs. The rabbits were bobbing in their hundreds in the meadows by the woods; high in the sky a buzzard hung and wheeled against the milky blue, and I heard this mewing cry answered by another in the distance.

With the increase in mechanization and factory farming many sounds which were common are not so today – the crowing of cocks and the cackling of hens; the rattle of buckets and the swish of the milk into the pail from whitewashed cow-sheds lit by the golden light of a stable lantern in winter; the important 'Clook! Clook!' of a hen with chicks as she walked slowly across the yard, her feathers puffed out and her wings slightly spread so that she looked like a ship sailing before the wind, the chicks running and cheeping in all directions; the gobbling of the turkey cock and the plaintive sound of the poults; the sudden skirling of a flock of guinea-fowl and their cry, 'Go back! Go back!'; the squealing of pigs as they heard the farmer coming to feed them, followed by a sudden silence, broken only by their guzzling when the troughs were filled. One sound that I always loved was the clatter of hooves on the stones of the yard, as the great draft horses were led out of the stables to be harnessed to cart or wagon. I liked to hear the voices of the men talking to the horses and to see the little wandering yellow lights of the lanterns, especially in the winter when the moon shone bright on a clear morning and if one listened one could hear the bark of a dog fox. All these and many more were daily sounds, I am tempted to say natural sounds, which have been replaced by the roar of the tractor, and they were heard against a background of silence, the stillness of a countryside when cars and aeroplanes were scarcely known.

There is a sound which I have not heard for many years – the rolling of the nightjars, or goat-suckers as they were called locally, on hot summer nights, together with their soft shadowy flight and the sharp clap of their wings as they chased each other in the dusk. As I lay in bed before dropping off to sleep it was this sound that I heard – a steady churring which went on and

on with sudden changes in key. Nothing expresses the stillness
of those summer nights more than this sound.

Down at the bottom of the hill, on the opposite side of the
lane to the woods, lay some marshy meadowland. Here I have
heard snipe drumming in the display period in the spring, their
wild erratic flight suddenly turning into a swift dive, with the
goat-like bleating sound caused by the air rushing through the
spread outer tail feathers. I heard this sound in Iceland during
the Second World War. Though I was at that time in a strange
rocky landscape by the sea, with no vegetation but rock plants
and grasses, and though this sound was mingled with that of
whimbrel, arctic tern and many sea birds and plover, yet it
transported me straight back to my green valley in Sussex.

In the woods were many sounds, each belonging to its time
and season. The harsh scream of the jay and the chatter of the
magpie; the shrill laugh of the green woodpecker, the yaffle or
eackle, alternating with his staccato rapping in the trees, this
sound varying according to the nature of the wood. Sometimes
it was a hard ringing sound, sometimes on a soft patch of rotten
wood it would be more muffled and interspersed with short
sharp notes.

One of the most beautiful sounds of all was the hum of
myriads of insects in the woods on a hot day. I would lie on a
mossy bank and listen until my ears became attuned to the
incessant murmur, until it resolved itself into individual sounds
heard against the general roar: the zoom of a bumble-bee as it
climbed out of a flower in its peculiar clumsy way; the busy hum
of honey-bees among flowers or high among the blossom of
chestnuts or limes; the sudden, almost alarming 'Pee-ee-ee!' of
a hover-fly close to one's ear; the churring of grasshoppers. So
still was the air in the deep woodlands that the tumbling of a
stag-beetle among dry leaves, or the rustling scamper of a shrew
would make me start, and I could hear the rasping noise made
by a foraging wasp as a positive sound.

A sound which I suppose few young people today can have
heard is the sound, together with the motion and vibration, of
driving in a pony trap. Perhaps I am being met at a little country
station. The train puffs away into the distance; outside in the
station yard stands the trap. The sun beats down so that the

seats are warm. As I put my foot on the step it gives a little. I am now thinking of a particular journey. First the horse would start to move out of the station yard with the harness creaking. A steady pull up a small hill followed. At the top of the hill came a level part then a gentle downward slope. Here came a clucking from the driver, a flick of the reins on the horse's back and the twitch of his tail. The walk changed to a trot, the hoofs going 'Clip! Clop!' on the stony road, the wheels vibrating through the seat. Then for a spell the crunching rumble of the wheels; the sound of the horse's hoofs; the jolting and swaying of the trap; the creak and jingle of the harness mixed with the smell of the horse, the smell of the harness, of the cushions in the warmth of the sun; the pleasant burring talk of the driver; glimpses of cottage gardens over hedges; of the fields and woods on every side; these all became parts of one sensation. After trotting along a hot sunny stretch of road we would enter a deep tunnel of green shade through woodland. Here the sounds altered; the clop of the hoofs and the rumble of the wheels were softened by the leaves, moss and damp earth on the road and by the thick canopy of trees. Presently we would reach a steep hill, where we got out and walked to ease the horse; then, at the top, we were off again at a brisk trot; and all the while there was time – time to talk, time to look, time to shout greetings over the hedge, to smell the smells and hear the sounds, to be part of a rural whole.

I cannot leave sounds without mentioning one more. In our ancient church there was a very old barrel organ which an old man played before and after service in the gallery at the west end. Sometimes in the strangest situations the tune that he played has come into my mind. In the Second World War, for instance, I would suddenly hear it in my subconscious mind, with the groaning and creaking as the handle was turned, and I was a small boy waiting for the services to begin once more.

People

I THINK very few people today, except those of my own generation, can appreciate quite how much rural England has changed in the last seventy years. It is not a question of knowing the facts but of having lived at that time, of belonging emotionally to a former period.

There is one special way in which this change is marked. When I was a boy the difference between town and country, between townsfolk and countryfolk, was almost so great as to divide the land into two. To go from a town into the country at that time was not merely to exchange streets and houses for lanes, hedges and cottages, it was to enter another world, to find oneself among people whose whole way of life and habit of mind, whose speech and even whose clothes were completely different from those of townsfolk. The phrase 'living in the country' had scarcely been invented; people were either urban or rural.

It is impossible, of course, to draw a line and say 'here the change began'. Change had been coming slowly since the early beginnings of the Industrial Revolution. In his remarkable book, *English Social History*, G. M. Trevelyan, noting the effect that the importation of cheap, mass-produced wheat from the United States into England had in the nineteenth century, writes, 'An even more important consequence has been the general divorce of Englishmen from life in contact with nature, which *in all previous ages* had helped to form the mind and the imagination of the island race.'

I believe that Trevelyan has touched on the heart of the matter. When I have spoken of the changes that have come about in my lifetime, I have often been told that they were not so much changes as stages in evolution. I think such a belief shows a misunderstanding, for what has occurred has not been simply a change in emphasis but a revolution, I would say a profound change, not just in outward things but in the very nature of people. The people, even in rural parts, have changed from a rural tradition to an urban one, even the younger members of old rural families. There has been, as Trevelyan says, 'a general divorce of Englishmen from life in contact with nature'.

To emphasize my belief I will quote from another book of interest to those who feel, as I do, that the change is of the greatest importance, *The Days that We Have Seen* by George Ewart Evans.

After quoting in his turn from the writings of C. S. Lewis, the author writes,

> But roughly speaking we may say that whereas all history was for our Ancestors divided into two periods, the pre-Christian and the Christian, and to two only, for us it falls into three — the pre-Christian, the Christian, and what may reasonably be called the post-Christian. This surely must make a momentous difference.

And he goes on to say that he is not regarding these periods merely from a theological point of view.

> I am considering them simply as cultural changes. When I do that it appears to me that the second change is even more radical than the first. Christians and pagans had much more in common with each other than either has with a post-Christian. The gap between those who worship different gods is not so wide as that between those who worship and those who do not.

I believe this to be true, but I must emphasize the fact that I do not believe that all old-fashioned country folk were simple, pious Christians and all townsfolk were not. Such a belief would be sentimental and false, as I know very well from experience. It is rather that the old rural people had an awareness of, and belief in, natural forces of which the modern urban dweller is unaware.

The fact is that, as an urban way of life and habit of mind has replaced a rural one, it has become impossible to speak of natural evolution. What we have seen during this century is the end of a rural mentality and the beginning of an urban one, which implies the end of a people who have an awareness of natural forces, a purely instinctive awareness, and their replacement by a people whose religion has become a belief in technology and a life increasingly devoted to a search for an ever-higher material standard of living.

In case my opinion appears to be too sweeping, or too harsh, I will quote from Evans once more. 'There comes from the rural communities in Britain and Ireland a strong confirmation that the changes of recent times are not simply the quantitative changes that accrue gradually from century to century but the prologue to a new epoch.'

I have always been grateful for the fact that when I was a boy much of the old rural way of life still survived, and I was fortunate in experiencing it.

There is one great change which I cannot help feeling is not always apparent to many people; this is the fundamental change in village life. For hundreds of years villages, and village life, were, so to speak, organic. People lived in villages because they had been born there, as had their fathers and grandfathers for many generations, or because their trade or craft was necessary to the village. The land-owner, the farmer great or small, the farm labourer, the blacksmith, the thatcher, the builder, right down to the humblest villager, they were all as much part of the place as were the fields or the houses. Even the parson or the schoolmaster, even if they came from outside, became an essential part of the village and its life. When I was a boy it was still common to find country parsons who had lived in their villages so long that they were regarded as a permanent part of village life. They had christened, prepared for Confirmation, married, christened the children of the marriages and finally buried the members of their flock, as long as most could remember; and this gave an extraordinary sense of continuity. As mobility has increased, as village schools have been closed and the children educated centrally, so there has been both a greater flight from the village and a greater influx from the outer world. The result has been a complete change in village life. As more and more of the old people die off, so the sense of local life and continuity disappears with them.

One of the best rural books of recent times is Flora Thompson's *Lark Rise to Candleford*. Its virtue lies in its simplicity and its understanding of a way of life which was her own; and to me it seems that its greatest virtue is that it is not distorted or overweighted with political or social theories or swamped by bogus 'simple life' philosophies.

She makes her attitude clear in another book which she wrote, *A Country Calendar*, of life in Heatherley (or Grayshott) on the Surrey–Hampshire border.

> In agricultural countries, such as that of Laura's birth, people were still much as they had been in her childhood. Those born on the land with very few exceptions, lived and died on the land . . . The old family names survived generation after generation in the villages, and the very fields with their customary rotation of crops helped to confirm the feeling of continuity.

She had changed rural life for rural suburbia.

> In Heatherley, few who lived there had been born in the place or had lived there as children. Having broken with their own personal past and come to a place without traditions, the villagers appeared to live chiefly for the passing moment. The past, especially the country past, was nothing to them, and if they looked forward to a future, it was a future of change – to the good time which newspaper prophets assured them was to come with the new century, when new machinery would be invented to do the work and man, with unlimited leisure, would live on a tabloid diet at the cost of a penny a day.

At the time of which I am writing a man's life and his work were accepted as natural things, two halves of a whole.

As I am writing about the country people whom I knew in Sussex it may seem strange that I should begin by describing a German. This man was a prisoner of war working for the

Farmer family, who owned the shop. I remember him as a peasant type, weather-beaten, with the kind of simple, scowling face that peasants so often have, a face which comes from peering into the sun, the wind and rain, for a lifetime so that the elements leave their marks as they do on stone or wood. You will never see this face in a town. I have known the same kind of face among countrymen in England and you may see such a face, though an older one, in Pieter Brueghel's painting of a shepherd. My sister and I liked him instinctively, as children do, and we used to go with him in the farm tumbril to fetch logs and faggots from the woods. I remember how the wheels of the tumbril crunched on the road and how it rocked and jolted along the woodland tracks, sometimes going deep into a rut so that we were nearly thrown out, sometimes jolting over a stone; the horse plodding on with his great hairy feet; the creak of the harness; the smell of the horse in the hot sunshine; the whisk of his tail when the flies bothered him. The German stood with his legs apart swaying as the tumbril rocked, holding the reins, chewing a piece of grass, flicking at the flies with a switch and clucking to the horse. He could speak no English and we no German but we understood each other perfectly. There were we, two small English children; there was he, a German peasant wrenched away from his home, his farm, his beloved country; forced first to carry a rifle and shoot Englishmen; then to wear the prisoner-of-war uniform with a red patch sewn on – a circle, so I was told, over a vital part, to act as a target if he escaped. Round us was the English countryside, probably very like his own: the sun was hot, the woods were green and cool; the birds sang; the butterflies flitted from flower to flower. The air was full of the pungent scents of summer; the foxgloves grew everywhere, spire behind spire of beautiful purple flowers, spotted and flecked with an exquisite pattern, bumble-bees blundering and booming inside the bells. On the beaten-earth road scarlet pimpernels were open wide in the sun; wild pansies and wild strawberries grew in open patches; rabbits bobbed among the hazels and small shrews squeaked and rustled among fallen leaves.

We three, the German in his prison uniform and us two children, were in a little sun-baked world cut off from the outer world. If one stood still one could hear the throbbing beat of gunfire from France, where men, German and English who wished each other no harm, were slaughtering each other in a weltering carnage; making a living hell of the green earth. Why? Because of empires and high finance and power politics and greed. Was the world not big enough and beautiful enough for us all? And we, English and Germans alike, knew that our cause was just and God was on our side.

Just above our cottage the little shop lay back from the road in a kind of small square. On the left a cottage stood upon a bank approached by steps. Here lived a family called Cobble. The husband was a kind of man who was very common in the Sussex countryside in those days. When I say 'very common' I do not mean lacking in individuality but that in a physical sense there were certain types in country places. He was of medium height, rather bleached or clay-coloured in his general appearance, with pale greyish-brown hair and moustache. He was, as they all were, weathered by constant exposure to wind and rain and sunshine. Another kind, in a physical sense, had the same clay-brown face with no red in it but with very dark brown hair. If I remember correctly the eyes of the first kind were grey-blue; of the second, brown. Just occasionally one may see men, and women, who still show these characteristics in the more remote country places; but they are growing steadily fewer. Mr Cobble's wife was a little woman with dark hair which was pulled back tightly, parted in the middle and rolled into a bun at the back. Her hair was either black or very dark and she always made me think of a Dutch doll of a kind which was common then, being made of wood with a round face and black hair painted on the head with a parting in the middle. The common speech was full and burring, except in some of the women who had rather shrill voices. In the men it was soft, low in tone, with a full insistence on the letter R, and 'I' pronounced as a strong 'OI'. There was, especially with this little woman, a tendency to pronounce 'Th' as D – 'Dat as idden' or 'Tidden'. The general effect was very rural, a pleasant soft burring whole, sometimes the sounds being run together so that it was difficult for a stranger to understand. I believe that, even now, I could tell where a man comes from by the way he pronounces 'I', from the full south country 'OI' to the soft Welsh 'AI', almost 'AYE' in Shropshire, or the hard West Riding 'AH' – a sound which is impossible to write.

The women commonly had the same clayey-brown appearance and frequently rather deep-set eyes, blue-grey or brown. One may see just this type of face in the paintings of George Clausen. I have a drawing of a Warwickshire woman which I did before the Second World War which is a good example of the kind of face that I am trying to describe. There was something in their faces which made them quite unlike, not only the faces of town people, but the vast majority of faces today. It is difficult to define, but I think it is most noticeable in the expression of the eyes and the mouth; there is a closeness to the soil in the whole expression of the face which has nearly vanished.

One of the greatest changes is in people's clothes. Then men's working clothes consisted almost invariably of a washed-out white or striped flannel shirt, not open at the neck or with an attached collar, but a shirt with no collar and usually with a stud in the neck band; the coloured open-necked shirt or one with an attached collar was unknown. In summer in particular the sleeves were rolled up to show weather-beaten arms, and a waistcoat was worn, sometimes open, sometimes buttoned up. Trousers, often of corduroy, were worn with braces, sometimes a leather belt as well, and it was common to see them tied below the knee with string or a strawband or a strap as they tended to be on the long side. Their thick, heavy boots were usually greased and not blacked. Boys were dressed in a similar manner but they often wore corduroy knee-breeches on the long side and buttoned loosely below the knee.

The women and girls wore long-skirted dresses and usually boots. The dresses were made of some warm material in winter, or cotton in summer, very often with white aprons or coloured pinafores. The women wore their hair pulled back in a bun, and the girls mostly had long hair, sometimes tied back, sometimes plaited or worn with a snood. The jeans, windbreakers and anoraks which one sees today were never seen. They mostly wore long stockings and strong boots; they had to be strong, weatherproof and designed for walking.

At the shop lived old Mr and Mrs Farmer and Miss Farmer, a niece, who ran the shop. A grandson of the old couple, called Robert, drove the high trap or dog-cart with a very fast trotting pony of which he was extremely proud. In this he delivered the groceries; and he went once a week to the little market town, where he would execute special orders.

Mr and Mrs Farmer were elderly, to me very old. They were the parents and grandparents of innumerable Farmers who lived locally. Mr Farmer had some trouble with his breathing so he snorted and grunted a great deal which, as his speech was broad and burring and he spoke from the depths of beard and whiskers, made him difficult to understand. He had a considerable frontage and walked with a staff, coming along in a deliberate four-square way. There was something of the patriarch about him; he used many old-fashioned words and phrases. 'Ap you doan' 'ear me!' he would shout waving his stick at the trespassing boy or girl, 'ap' being short for 'happen'. In my time he did no work, being past much activity, but was always about, thumping along with his stick. He had a rough tongue at times but would occasionally greet me with 'Mornin' squire!' in a jovial, breathy way when he was in a good humour.

The old lady was bent, like a little old mouse, a character out of Beatrix Potter. She expressed herself commonly, as so many of the folk did, in Biblical language. 'Ah', she would say, 'we spend our lives thinking of the belly; and all that goes into the belly passes out into the draught!' This had a peculiar significance for me because, in common with everyone else, we had an outdoor privy with a wooden seat with a hole in it. When the wind blew the draught was so strong that the lighter form of toilet paper refused to go down the hole but sailed up to the roof.

The little shop was of a kind which was common at that time in country places. The door opened with the clang of a bell, and one entered a small space in front of a counter amid a profusion of things. There were sacks of corn, and middlings for chicken mash; buckets, wood choppers, dippers, saucepans and kettles; balls of string, hanks of clothes line, cards on which were fixed little boxes, packets and bottles of iodine, castor oil, boracic, cough mixture, lint, bottles of ink, pens, pencils and pieces of rubber. On the shelves were writing materials, blocks of paper, packets of envelopes and mysterious things called 'writing compendiums'. These consisted of a folding container, inside which was a pad of paper, two packets of envelopes and a pencil. They were often decorated on the outside with pictures of flowers and sometimes raised patterns or letters in shiny gold. Then there were notebooks, plain or ruled for cash, and, according to the season, skipping ropes, whiptops and other odds and ends. Some things were on the floor, some on the counter, some stacked in shelves, many hung from hooks in the ceiling. In those days ordinary groceries were not sold in packets; we bought sugar, soda, butter, lard, bacon or cheese by weight. Bacon was cut on a board with a large knife, cheese by a piece of wire with a wooden handle at each end. I was always fascinated to see the wire pulled through the cheese and longed to do it myself. The buying of sugar, tea, sweets or other such commodities was quite a ceremony. Sweets were kept in large glass jars – which frequently bore the legend '4 oz. 1*d*'; indeed 2*d* or 3*d* for '4 oz.' was venturing into big money. As well as sweets there were rainbow-coloured suckers on sticks which changed colour as you sucked them, and sherbert dabs – ovals of toffee on a stick which you stuck in the sherbert powder then licked. Or there was another kind, with a liquorice tube inserted into the top of a small bag. The powder was sucked up through the tube. If you sucked too hard the sherbert flew into the back of your throat and brought on a great fit of coughing and gasping. Among the sweets which I have not seen for many years were twisted sticks of barley sugar, and sticks of another kind, which were made of stripes of brilliant colours, red, green, yellow of an almost poisonous-looking brilliance and flavoured strongly with aniseed. I did not really like aniseed, but as these were cheap and lasted a long time I persuaded myself that I did. One advantage was that if I wrapped a paper bag round the end I could hold them to suck, or lay them down to be finished later if I had had enough. In those days the amount of dust or other 'foreign bodies' which they collected did not worry us.

If I wanted '4 oz.' of boiled sweets, Miss Farmer would put her hand into one of the tall glass bottles, grasp a handful and then drop them with a clinking sound into a brass scoop on the scales, until the other side with little lead weights rose level with the scoop. Usually when it did so she dropped another one in for luck. One of the most fascinating performances was over the weighing of toffee. This was in large, jagged pieces which she held in the palm of one hand and then deftly cracked with a toffee hammer.

The buying of sugar or similar items was quite an elaborate ceremony. The sugar was kept in a wooden container, rather like a bookcase divided into partitions with a piece of wood along the bottom to prevent it from falling out. It was scooped out with a tool like a small shovel or coal scoop, and weighed in the brass scoop on the scales. A piece of thick blue paper was placed on the counter, then gathered up, twisted neatly into a cone, and the sugar tipped into it. Finally the spare paper at the top was folded over and tucked in like a lid. There is a sensuous pleasure to be had from watching this ceremony, the scooping of the brown demerara sugar with its soft, moist texture and its rich smell, the way it is poured into the conical bag and the feel and weight of the bags. Conical bags of this kind were used for many groceries. Square wads of paper of different colours, blue for sugar, brown or grey for other items, hung from nails by a string through a corner, each sheet being pulled off as it was needed. Sugar, washing soda, sweets or tea, scooped out, weighed, and finally handed over the counter in a conical bag, seemed quite different to such things bought in ready-made cartons or plastic bags; one had a sense of their being 'merchandise' in the romantic sense of the word, as when one reads of 'spices' in the Bible.

Among the many things in the shop were brightly coloured pictures of smiling people rubbing themselves with someone's liniment or using someone's soap or corn cure. There was one of a maid in cap and apron turning, with her hand on the door as she went off to bed, and saying, 'Goodnight' to whatever the product was, 'You do the washing while I go off to bed', and one famous one of a dirty tramp writing a letter, 'Dear Sir, six months ago I used your soap. Since then I've used no other.' There were pictures of rosy-faced ploughmen puffing contentedly at 'Country Life' tobacco as they followed the plough, and of a man dreaming over a pipe with some kind of beautiful

picture in the cloud of smoke, the caption being 'Such fair
visions you only see when smoking pipes of BDV.' There was
one advertisement for waterproof dubbin; as we always called
the domestic staff 'dubbins' at my school this seemed to me
exquisitely funny. Behind the counter, almost lost among suspended saucepans and cards, was the face of Miss Farmer
– known as Margie. In all the years I knew her I cannot remember her other than smiling and in a good temper. She was a good
Chapel woman, of a type that one seldom sees now. And
unifying the whole was an indescribable smell, compounded of
bacon, cheese, candles, paraffin, herbs, onions, coffee, sweets
and countless other things.

It was not only a shop but a bakehouse and a small farm.
From here we bought our milk, butter and cream, our bread,
and a special kind of cake which never varied. It was made in a
round tin, and had currants and sultanas inside, a rough craggy
top and a flavour all of its own. In addition we could have a joint
and potatoes roasted in the bakehouse or milk puddings. I have
never tasted such barley-kernel puddings anywhere else. The
slow, steady heat of the brick oven, fired by faggots of wood,
was the perfect way to cook a milk pudding without drying it
up. The bread was fine crusty stuff, such as one scarcely sees
today; the milk was thick with cream and the butter as yellow as
a primrose, with a life in the texture and a taste which seem to
have vanished.

The old couple's son, father of Robert, was mostly busy with
the farm. He was as Biblical in his speech as his parents. If you
greeted him, 'Good morning, Mr Farmer, your roses look well',
he would answer, 'Ah! all things come in their time. June be the
month of roses as spring be the time of the singing of birds and
autumn the time of corn harvest. All things work together for
good, each in his time and season.' One winter night when the
stars were very bright I found him looking up at the sky. 'That
star up there,' he said, 'that be the pole star; and them bright
ones, that's Orion', (he pronounced it '*Orion*').

'When I consider thy heavens, the work of thy fingers, the
moon and the stars, which thou hast ordained;

What is man, that thou art mindful of him? and the son of
man, that thou visitest him?'

I have heard him and many others say things and use a turn of phrase that would seem suspect, a kind of affectation, to many people today if I wrote them down, yet then they were natural, everyday speech. This Biblical turn of speech was, I think, one of the things which make that time seem so remote. The words which we heard in church, the beautiful language of the Authorized Version of the Bible, seemed in no way strange, but part of our lives. As one stood looking over a ploughed field in autumn, the air pungent with newly turned earth, the furrows shining from the plough share, the plough pulled by magnificent horses; or as one saw the same field in full blade with a bloom of blue-green health upon it; or finally the ears thick and golden, murmuring under the September sun like the company of the blessed, one could express oneself easily and naturally in the language of the Bible, 'The smell of my son is as the smell of a field which the Lord hath blessed.'

When I heard the choir singing at Harvest Festival, 'The valleys also shall stand so thick with corn, that they shall laugh and sing', the imagery was not remote. The fields and hills stretched away on every hand as we came out of church, ripe and fruitful under the golden sun of late summer.

Some time ago I borrowed a book of photographs of life in the Yorkshire dales in the early years of this century. It was by two ladies, one of whom was the photographer and one who had written the text. Soon after it was published I heard some critics discussing it on the radio. They appeared to be fairly young men. I was struck by their general attitude and particularly by one aspect of it. One of them, describing the people in the photographs, spoke of the worn, almost brutish appearance of the people, the farmers, farm-workers, saddlers, bakers, blacksmiths, the real inhabitants of those dales. The attitude revealed by their remarks was, to me, startling, indeed horrifying. It seemed to me an urban, a modern, misinterpretation. I had been greatly moved by the same photographs because in the worn, weatherbeaten faces I saw nothing degraded; I saw people whom I felt I knew, people whose outlook on life, whose whole scale of values was in tune with my own. I cannot possibly understand or sympathize with the modern idea that hardworking lives, lived against such a background of weather, old-fashioned farming and country standards were in any way limited or degraded. I found this book very moving precisely because the people in the photographs were the counterpart of the people whom I knew.

A deaf and dumb woman worked in the house at the back of the shop. She was a cheerful soul in spite of her affliction. She lived in a cottage up the road with her brother and a sister who was also deaf and dumb. This brother was one of a pair of men, Jim and George, whom I always seemed to meet together, trudging to work in the morning or home again in the evening. Jim was a tall, angular man who loped along, staff in hand, like a pair of bent compasses. George, was short and stocky, as round of body and face as Jim was long. As I remember they never looked around but plodded along the stony lanes, their boots making a steady crunching noise; and although the one was so tall and the other so short they kept a steady pace together. It was common in those days to meet men walking because even bicycles were not plentiful. I remember one man who had a three-speed gear which seemed a thing of wonder. But most of the men trudged at a steady pace, never appearing to alter their speed up hill or down, no matter how steep the gradient. In stormy weather they often carried enormous, faded blue umbrellas — gig umbrellas we called them — with club-shaped wooden handles. The spread of these was so great that they would keep a man dry in a downpour. Every morning during the week men would pass our cottage on their way to work, sometimes going several miles, and in the evening they would return. As I lay in bed I would hear the sound of heavy boots with a steady 'Crunch! Crunch!' growing out of the distance, growing louder as they passed and dying away again. The boots were large, heavy ones with hob-nails and iron toes and heels, making a special sound on the stony roads before the time of tarmac. The sound of trudging boots and the low burring murmur of their voices expressed the slow, unhurrying pace of those days.

Above us, on the opposite side of the lane, was a double cottage looking across the valley. In the further one lived two elderly maiden ladies, the Misses Cobble, whose home was spotless and who, in spite of a certain primness of manner were kind, hospitable people. Sometimes if we had visitors they would put them up for us. My elder sister told me of an occasion on which one of the visitors upset a jug of water. In order to mop it up they rolled back the carpet. She never forgot the clean, scrubbed, 'snow-white' boards that this revealed.

The little bedrooms were perfect cottage rooms, but I must stress, as I did in writing of the gardens, that they were in no way 'artistic' or self-conscious but simply the real thing. Most of the room was taken up by a bedstead with brass rails at the head and the foot, a feather mattress making it high from the floor. They were covered with white, honeycombed bedspreads with a special smell. The rest of the room was filled by a chair and a wash-stand, with a piece of carpet beside the bed. The top of the stand held a flowered china basin, which fitted into a hole, beside it was a pot for tooth brushes, a soap dish and a bottle and glass of water for cleaning the teeth. A ewer stood in the basin filled with soft water smelling of rain; and underneath was a chamber-pot to match. On the walls hung framed texts and coloured pictures of the Royal Family, or some famous figure, or a special kind of coloured print, often of children in many-flounced dresses or velvet suits accompanied by collie dogs or St Bernards. Sometimes the children were picking wild flowers in meadows among lambs; sometimes they were skating or sliding on frozen ponds or snowballing, or they might be coming home from church or singing carols. Some of the pictures were of a special religious sort, perhaps of a girl lying prostrate on a tombstone or of a returning prodigal welcomed home by his aged parents. There was often in these cottage bedrooms a kind of picture which was given by the Sunday School. They were simple and direct in their theology and, to me, rather frightening. One, for instance, was crowded with figures like a crude Brueghel. It was called, *The Straight and Narrow Way and The Crooked Way*. On the straight way were shown figures toiling upwards to Heaven. On the other, groups of wicked idlers were dallying as they went, apparently unaware of the red glow of the Infernal Regions which awaited them at the end of the road. To wake to such a picture could be very unnerving – especially if I knew I had taken an apple from someone's orchard or a spoonful of sugar from the cupboard on the sly.

There might be a small shelf with a few books, probably Sunday school prizes, with titles like *Winning the Victory, The Mad Ruthvens* and *The Flower Fadeth*.

The fields, meadows and woods seen through the little curtained windows, the sound of chickens cackling, sheep bleating, cows lowing, swallows twittering under the eaves, seemed to take on a peculiar intensity. A bowl of cowslips or primroses on the window-sill completed the picture, creating in some almost forgotten way a kind of country perfection.

The old ladies liked to talk to us and we to them. Their prim, quiet speech was full of Sussex phrases. On a warm summer evening they would say it had been a lovely day, 'but the flies do terrify one so'. This word, and some others, had a special inflexion that made it unlike the same words used in common speech elsewhere.

One memory comes back to me and I have been trying to think why it should have been. It went with a feeling of happy tiredness and a tingling of the skin after a long day out of doors, and the coolness of the sheets. As I lay, half asleep, the dusk deepening and the sounds one by one ceasing till all was still, I was conscious of the murmuring of voices from below. I think it was because the rooms had very thin ceilings so that people could be heard talking through the floor-boards.

Next door to the old ladies lived a family, father, mother and a small boy younger than us, called Billy. Billy's father was a dark man with an almost gypsy touch about him. He had a very white row of false teeth, which he would exhibit in a white flash of a smile. His grandfather, who lived further down the hill, was a big old man with white hair and beard who walked with a ceremonial slowness, using a long ash staff. He loved to talk; when you met him it was best to greet him without stopping if you did not want to be caught. His way was to stand still and then begin a complicated movement using his two feet and his staff, by means of which he swung round to face you; and once you were caught there was little chance of getting away. Billy walked beside him, a miniature edition of his grandfather, square walk, staff and all, an exact copy of the old man with all his mannerisms. Sometimes if you met him alone he would pass on with a wag of his head, just like the old man. If you said, 'Are

you busy, Billy?', he would reply in a portentous manner, 'Ah!
Got some jobs on!' and there was no delaying him. He liked to
come and visit us, and he would remark on what we were doing
with all the air of an ancient gaffer. 'I see you be washing your
curtains', he would say, or, 'I expect you noticed my new
boots!' One day when he came round we had some bananas,
which he eyed with obvious longing. 'What be them funny
things?' he said, adding, 'You take one and eat it for yourself!' I
began to eat one and he wagged his head in a knowing manner.
'Ah!', he said, 'Lil' gal doyed along o' them!' He beamed with
delight when we gave him one.

When a new baby sister arrived he was very concerned and
rather bewildered by all the to-do. 'Well, Billy,' said my sister
when he came down one morning, 'How is the new baby?' 'Ah,'
he said, 'She's all roight, but,' with a note of exasperation in his
voice, 'they keep on shuttin' the door y' know!'

High on the opposite side of the valley, right among the
woods, stood a cottage by itself, where lived a gamekeeper's
widow and her daughter, Sally. We often played with Sally,
who was rather older than us; I remember how indignant she
was when my father referred to her as a child. She had a
gramophone with records of Harry Lauder singing 'Roamin' in
the Gloamin'', 'Risin' Early in the Mornin'', and other songs
which we would listen to if it was wet. It was one of the early
forms of gramophone with a horn, and you wound it up by a
handle at the side. There was a swing outside, placed on the side
of a steep slope so that when you swung forwards you appeared
to be flying among the trees; I cannot think of it now without a
feeling in the pit of my stomach, half-pleasure and half-fear.
Sometimes if we played with a ball it would be lost among the
bracken which grew everywhere; we would hunt for it all round
the place where we had seen it last without finding it, and Sally
would say, 'Oi reckon 'e's just 'ere somewhere a' *larfin*' at us!'
Sally, like many country girls, was frightened of thunder and
when there was a storm she would sit in a cupboard with her
fingers in her ears.

One man whom I remember from watching him with his
horses was the head carter on the estate. He was a small man,
and as I remember him he seemed to stand with his feet a little

apart planted firmly on the ground in large heavy boots, leaning forward a little, with the butt of his long carter's whip on the ground held as though it were a staff. He wore a weathered felt hat and a rather long jacket of an old cut. I think his trousers were of corduroy as was common, and he wore leggings. He had a curious shambling way of walking which came from following horses on heavy wet land or behind a plough, a walk which I think you will never see now, a walk which however clumsy it may have appeared he could nevertheless keep up all day as few could do now.

His face below the brim of his battered hat was weather-beaten with a long nose and a rather underhung lower lip; indeed he had the appearance of being an awkward, sullen-tempered man. Whether this was so I do not know, but it did not extend to his horses. The great thing that I remember was a remarkable sympathy, one might almost say a kind of communication, between him and the beautiful giants with which he worked. Indeed I know of nothing more beautiful than a team of draught horses with their noble heads, their splendid shoulders and quarters and their great shaggy feet.

I remember one occasion when they were felling timber. The men were stripping off the branches from a large tree. The carter stood in his characteristic pose, and the horses hitched one behind the other waited patiently, their heads drooping a little as though in a doze. The tree was ready to be lugged away, the team was hitched to it and the carter stood a little ahead and to one side. He uttered a peculiar long-drawn sound. The horses suddenly woke to a kind of expectant unison; they leaned forward into their collars and braced their great muscles; another peculiar cry and the whole magnificent team came into action with a concerted heave. The communication between the carter and his team seemed so perfect that they had the appearance of working as one united being, using the maximum of strength with the minimum of waste. It must be over sixty years since I saw this, but it has made an indelible impression on me.

At one time I had a little white kid which I had reared with a bottle. It went everywhere with me. It would come into the cottage, and if I shut the door it would jump in through the window. Unfortunately it would also do things indoors which are best done in the open. It became very playful and I have seen it outside our garden gate entertaining a group of children on their way to school with all sorts of antics: leaping in the air; standing on its forefeet; dancing along on its hind legs; butting the children. These children often walked several miles to school never having heard of a school bus. In winter they wore strong boots and thick, hand-knitted stockings. They took their lunch with them — bread, bacon, cheese, and a mild, home-brewed beer which everyone drank, young and old. The schoolmaster whom I remember was of a kind which has vanished — very much the sort whom I always imagine when I hear the word 'dominie'. I think he had no great learning — my father asked him once to give my sister and me some lessons but he would not undertake it as he said that he had no Greek or Latin; but I believe that the loss of these little village schools and of the old-fashioned village schoolmaster and mistress at their best is a very grievous loss. They counted so much in village life. Recently I saw a photograph of village children just at that time, which brought back another memory: they all wore hats and caps a good deal too large for them. We used to say it was because they were intended to last so long.

The Post Office up by the church was kept by the daughters of the estate bailiff. One of them was considered plain and the other pretty; my father said she looked like a startled fawn, but the plain one was the kinder of the two, the younger one seeming to me a bit sharp. If we went to draw money from our Post Office savings bank she would lecture us on spendthrift ways although we had our father's permission.

I remember two Rectors. One had been a missionary in the South Sea Islands or some such place. He and his wife were both Irish, and had no children but two little cairn terriers, one black and one mouse-coloured. I cannot remember the name of the black one, but the mouse-coloured one was called 'Banshee', which we were told was Irish for a ghost, and the little dog looked very like a ghost in the dusk. They were terrible rabbiters, and we seemed to spend a great deal of time searching in the woods with the Rector or his wife, calling 'Banshee! Banshee! Banshee!' The Rector was a great gardener and beekeeper, and specialized in roses. One day while he was working near the hives a bee stung him on the top of his bald head and his wife had to pull the sting out. He loved to get away in his garden but his wife would come and call for him if it was lunchtime or he was wanted in some way – she would stand on the lawn calling, 'Willie! Willie! Willie!' and he would mutter, 'Shan't!'

Once when he caught two boys stealing his apples he took them home and told their parents he had caught them red-handed. The boys howled and the mother went down on her knees and clasped one of them in her arms, saying, 'There now, Johnny, tell the Rector you didn't do it!'

The Rector and his wife loved the rectory and garden, it was one of those beautiful rambling rather shabby rectories which have been such a feature of our country life; but I think their hearts lay with their missionary work, and when he had re-covered from a severe breakdown they went back again.

The later Rector was a dignified white-haired, white-bearded old gentleman, an archdeacon, who had been headmaster of a well-known school. He treated everyone as though they were his pupil. Sometimes, during the singing of a hymn, he would beckon us out into the aisle and we would process behind him, round the church, out into the churchyard if it were fine, and back again. If I met him in the lane he would probably say, 'Now come with me and I will show you something.' There was a good chance that he would forget all about me, as he seemed to live in a higher atmosphere, but if he did not he would lead me to a patch of grass or a copse and point out a rare flower or some unusual object. 'There! Do you know what this is? That is a bee orchid. Do you see how the flower looks exactly like a bee?'

There were two 'big houses' in the village, the Hall, where the Squire lived, and the Place, where his agent lived – a man only less important than the Squire. The Squire and his family sat in a special pew where he could keep an eye on the rest of the congregation. He seemed to me a very old man with a bald head that sank a little in the middle. He was a kind man and a very good landlord, well thought of in the village; in his day many of the cottage rents were barely nominal. When he died one of his oldest tenants died at the same time, and the Rector spoke of the two old men, master and servant, passing on together after a full life.

We occasionally went to tea at both of these houses, though more frequently to the Place. The Hall stood near the church with a private door in the churchyard wall for the Squire and his family, and big wrought-iron gates to the drive. I remember going to tea there one winter day. The front door opened into an entrance hall where an enormous log fire burnt on a great open hearth with fire dogs. How much more than mere warmth a fire is, especially on this scale, imparting a spiritual as well as a physical warmth. The hall was full of the perfume of wood smoke.

One of the grandest occasions that I can recall was the wedding of the daughter of the Place, which took place in the church with the reception at the Hall. The bells fairly rocked the old church tower, and the organ boomed out the Wedding March as the distinguished looking couple walked down the aisle. The old Squire made a witty speech, in which he spoke of the bride's mother following hounds in a very dashing manner in a pony trap. He referred to Mary as 'The Flower that bloomed in the Place'. She was a charming girl, very kind to us children. She had a slight hesitation in her speech which was the result of overwork as a VAD in the First World War, but the hesitation in her speech went, strangely enough, with her charm and is always part of my memory of her.

Her mother was a nice old lady, very 'County' with a quaint, rather stiff smile and heavy lids which gave her eyes a hooded expression. We often sat behind her pew in church. She would turn round and beam at us, sometimes saying, 'Will you come to tea – come to tea! So nice!' She was fond of arranging rather grand picnics at which lots of 'young people' would play charades in the open air with a good deal of hilarity and shouting. Next Sunday she would turn round and beam at us again, saying, 'So glad you could come! So nice! Such a nice chawade!'

When we went to tea there it would be in the house in the winter or in cold weather, or in the garden in the summer when it was fine. We would have scones and white and brown bread and butter, cut very thin, apple and bramble jelly and several kinds of cake – spice cake, currant cake and a particular kind of chocolate cake with thick chocolate icing. Once we had some other children with us, one of whom was a small boy with a high-pitched voice and a punctilious manner. When he was offered some cake he said, 'I expect you have plenty more in the kitchen!' They were very kind, pleasant people and I remember these tea-parties as being extraordinarily happy occasions. On one occasion another boy, quite tiny, appeared with a large rose which he had picked in the garden, carrying it triumphantly with both hands like a trophy. It was perhaps a test of their kindness that they seemed to think it was a tremendous joke. We often came home with a great bunch of flowers from the lovely garden, or sometimes with fruit. One of our visits was on a Sunday. After tea we went to church with a quantity of gooseberries, some of which I had stuffed into the pockets of my shorts. During the service I became aware of an uncomfortable dampness, which by the time we started for home had resolved itself into two solid masses of squashed gooseberries.

Corn Harvest

ONE day, quite recently, I had been sketching a few miles from home. It was a perfect September day with a gentle blue sky, streaked with faint trails of white cirrus vapour. The sunshine was warm and golden as it is in those last days of a fine summer, after harvest. I ate my lunch in a stubble field leaning against a pile of straw warm, relaxed, saturated with sunshine, like a dozy old bee.

In this state of mental and physical relaxation I began to recall harvests which I had known many years ago. The part of Sussex where we lived was not a corn-growing district. There were none of the great fields of corn that one might have seen in East Anglia or that I have since seen in the flat land of the lower reaches of the Ouse or the plain of York. I remember one summer when the harvest was very good and the straw a particularly fine golden colour. It was in the country between Ripon and York that I saw a sight I have never seen since and I am unlikely to see again. The whole of that flat plain, as far as the eye could see, was cornfields. It was mostly cut and the fields were covered with stooks. I have never before or since seen so large an area all stooked at the same time, field behind field as far as the eye could see, with the stooks built in a variety of ways so that there was an infinite diversity of pattern. The conditions, the sky, the light, the settled weather, were perfect. The effect of the stooks over so wide an area made me think of the ribbed pattern of the linen smock such as countrymen used to wear.

Corn Harvest

In our deep-wooded country one would not see such a sight, but many farmers grew enough wheat, oats or barley for their own use: the farms were small mixed farms, and harvest time was as great a festival as haymaking.

I must be allowed the word 'festival' for that was how it was. No doubt many practical farmers today would reject the word with impatience. And yet, a young farmer spoke to me recently of harvest and a field of stooks having a mystical quality, a kind of symbolism.

At harvest festival the choir sang, 'O Lord, how manifold are thy works: in wisdom hast thou made them all'. May I not speak of mysticism and symbolism? I will write as I felt sitting in a stubble field in the September sunshine.

Stubble fields give me a pleasure which is only less than that of a field of ripe corn. The whole business of the harvest has a kind of symbolism, something I try to convey in painting. First the plough, the smell, colour and texture of the earth, the marvellous pungency of the newly turned furrows. I do not know how to convey the feeling caused in me by the lines of newly turned furrows except in painting. Then there come the young shoots, little green spikes among the brown, with the same indescribable effect of rhythmic lines. Later follow the full blue-green of the young corn, the swelling of the ears, the green turning more golden; and finally the field of ripe corn, warm and golden like a great bowl of treasure under the blue sky. Nothing quite equals this in its sense of complete fulfilment. For a perfect ending the corn must be stooked and stand in the September sunlight, echoing and completing the first rhythms of the plough.

Last of all comes the stubble. The corn is in: the air is the colour of honey, the stubble ranging from gold to bleached straw, the whole, with the smell of the straw in the warm air and the brushing of the short spines against one's feet, seems like a lull, a resting time, a time of complete stillness, before, once again, the plough travels through the waiting field turning up the rich brown earth. First there are the alternate strips of brown and gold; gradually the brown gains on the gold, until finally the field is brown again with a beauty of colour surface and rhythm like nothing else in the whole of nature.

Not long ago tractors came through this village, where I live now, with trailers loaded with straw bales. I could not help thinking how much we have lost of daily and seasonal pleasure with the march of 'progress'.

When the harvest was gathered the wagons, drawn by horses, would come along the narrow lanes to the farmyards, where the ricks were built. The ricks of wheat were often round, rather like a beehive with a thatched top, the butt ends of the sheaves being outwards so that they had a bristly appearance unlike a haystack. There is a farm within two miles of here where there lived a farmer who was proud of his skill in building such ricks. One day, some years ago, he was building some in his field and I did a sketch. He liked it and asked if I would do a larger painting for him from the sketch, which I did. He bought it from me and he has it now.

It used to be a splendid sight to see a rickyard filled with haystacks and cornricks. One of the finest I can remember seeing was during the Second World War when I was in Kent. The men who built and thatched them were proud of their skill, and would often decorate a round rick with a topknot and long ones with a kind of finial at each end made of straw.

As the wagons came down the lanes the straw would catch in the overhanging branches of trees, and some would lie on the ground in the gateways and in the yards, a beautiful bright gold against damp brown earth and green grass.

It seems natural that from thinking of harvest my mind should turn to barns. In our district I do not remember any of the great barns that one associates with a corn-growing district, but there were many small ones. I had a peculiar affection for them. Their interiors were like rustic churches, with the massive beams and rafters seen in the dim light or when the sun shone in through the great doors when they were open. The doors were large to allow wagons to be driven into the space in the centre so that the crops of hay or other things could be unloaded into the bays on either side.

When the bays were half-full they made wonderful places for reading on a wet day. I have often clambered up among the masses of soft, sweet-smelling hay and lain there deep in a book while the rain poured down outside. As I read I was conscious of the life of the farm going on round me. I would hear the clattering of a horse's hooves as it was led out of a stable to be hitched into a cart, the man's voice speaking to it, and then the rumble of the heavy wheels as he drove out of the yard. I would hear the lowing of cows from the pastures, the bleating of calves and then the rattle of a bucket as the farmer's wife gave them some milk and her voice speaking to them. Mixed with the steady falling of the rain came the keening of hens as they scratched among loose chaff and cavings in a Dutch barn. Further off I heard the scuttering sounds of ducks on the pond with a sudden '*Qu-a-a-ck*, quack, quack!', then the bark of the dog as a man came into the yard with a sack over his head against the rain. All the sounds were soothing, pleasant, softened by the thickness of the barn timbers and the muffling effect of the hay.

I would read on and on, lost in my book although dimly aware of outer things, until first a quietness and then a brightness made me look up. From a little shuttered window in the side of the barn I had a picture as in a frame, the darkness in the barn accentuating the brightness as the clouds parted and the sunlight streamed across the meadows, the distant woods and hills looking as fresh as if they had just been created. Then I would close my book and clamber down the ladder, out of the pungent dimness of the barn into the wet yard, from which steam was rising in the warmth of the sun, and stand there, a little sleepy, my hair full of bits of hay, blinking in the bright light.

I have already written of the rural landscape being created by and in turn helping to create the people who worked it and lived in it, but this was so at a time when the people, the landscape, the life, the sounds, even the weather were all parts of a whole. The completeness of which I was so aware and which I am trying to convey was of that time before great changes were obvious.

A few years ago when my wife and I were in Scotland we visited Cromarty, where we saw the birthplace of Hugh Millar, of whom I had never heard before. He was a stone-carver who became an eminent geologist, his interest in this subject being awakened by the great number of fossils to be found along the coast near his home.

I noticed a great difference in the response of my wife and myself to what we saw. She is greatly interested in geology and in collecting fossils and she was absorbed by the show-cases exhibiting his finds. My own interest was different; I was fascinated by the notes on his life; the photographs of Cromarty in his time, and of groups of fisherfolk; the beautiful old thatched cottage and all that spoke of the human side of his life and of the district. The fact is I have an actual dislike of geological formations, rocks, faults and the remains of prehistoric creatures, but as soon as there is human life my interest is aroused, especially by early forms of rural life, houses, tools and other such things. The blind forces of prehistoric times alarm me.

The picture those huge, fossilized skeletons conjures up seems to me anti-human. Indeed, I remember experiencing a similar fear of unknown and undefinable evil when I was taken as a boy to see the Imperial War Museum. I remember particularly the, to me, terrifying effect of a sombre-coloured dummy of a man hanging above me as though he was descending beneath a parachute.

I have written already of my fear when I saw the enormous black aeroplane on a murky evening when I was at boarding school.

Is my apprehension so fantastic? I do not think so, for it seems to me that a society increasingly divorced from nature, which places its faith more and more in the new forces created by technology, is in very great danger. I think that is why I am so aware of the hope that lies in Traherne's vision of felicity, and why I had so great a sense of satisfaction in the old-fashioned rural life that I love so much.

Traherne writes,

To conceive aright and to enjoy the world is to conceive the Holy Ghost and to see His love: which is the mind of the Father — For when you are once acquainted with the world, you will find the goodness and wisdom of God so manifest therein, that it was impossible another, or better, should be made. Which being made to be enjoyed, nothing can please or serve Him more, than the soul that enjoys it. For the soul doth accomplish the end of His desire in creating it.

But how can we enjoy the world, or delight in the goodness of God in creating it, or live with any hope, if we destroy it, if we pollute the earth on which we live and the very air which we breathe?

Walking

I REMEMBER a man to whom I was talking one day said to me, 'When I go into the country I notice one thing, a countryman always crosses the road diagonally; a townsman walks straight across. Can you tell me why that is?'

I think the answer is very simple although I doubt if it is quite so common today. In the days of which I am writing country roads were so quiet that one could hear a horse trotting or the rumbling of a cart a good way off, and its approach was so slow that country people did not acquire the habit of looking over their shoulders, they could cross a road without haste or danger.

We walked a good deal as most people did, for in such a place in those days one had to walk to get anywhere unless one owned a pony and trap or perhaps a bicycle. If we wanted a trap we hired one from Mr Farmer at the shop, but mostly we simply walked. I do not quite like writing, 'One had to walk', for we did it as a matter of course or for pleasure. Even we, the children, thought nothing of walking five miles into the little market town and five miles back and, as I have already said, the men mostly walked to and from work and the children to school. There was no hardship in it; it was natural and we enjoyed it.

I would say there is no better way to enjoy the countryside than to walk, particularly if one takes constant pleasure in what one sees and hears. One can see, one can hear, one can smell, and surely to be constantly seeing and constantly enjoying what one sees is a source of endless pleasure.

We quite often went for fairly long walks. In warm, fine weather we would take food with us so that we could spend a whole day out of doors. Often at teatime we would ask someone in a cottage, or farmhouse, to boil us a kettle so that we could make tea; or we would light a fire and boil our own kettle. Many of these stops were made at small isolated cottages where we found the people simple and friendly (I use the word 'simple' in its best sense), and they were usually very willing to make tea for us. Such a cottage might be in a little cultivated patch beside the wood. There would be a strip of vegetable garden, perhaps a little orchard or just one or two fruit trees, a piece of grass and some flowers in front of the cottage, and another strip with a few hens and ducks. The cottage and the garden were close under the wood, and a path probably led to a small stream where they had dug out a hole so that the water could accumulate. There was a rough stage of planks or some flat stones where one could dip one's bucket, and I always associate such a place with a large black kettle smelling of wood smoke being boiled on an open fire. I have had many cups of tea in such places, such tea as you will get nowhere else, compounded of spring water and the tang of wood smoke and new milk. The word 'pollution' had not been invented.

After we had walked a long way on a hot day such times were very pleasant. We would lie on the grass listening to the bees and the wood-pigeons crooning, the hens keening and a cockerel crowing; or we would cross over the brook by a plank bridge, out of the heat of the sun into a world of cool greens and browns flecked with brilliant splashes of sunlight. I would count such times among the happiest moments of my life, when I was happily tired, warmed with hot, sweet tea and rested.

The lanes by which we walked were narrow, white and stony, often very old lanes worn deep by centuries of use and by the action of water. In places they ran between high banks crowned with hawthorn hedges or arched over with trees. Often one passed a gate where a lane led into the woods, like a tunnel through the dense green of hazels, ashes and chestnuts, the ground a warm brown flecked with sunlight and the light shining down through the stems and branches, a dazzling maze of green, gold, blue and silver.

After the tea we would continue with a sense of refreshment. It cannot all have been fine weather; and yet, looking back, it seems to me that never were summer days so long, the sky so blue, the sunlight so golden, the people whom we met so smiling and pleasant. I would climb a little hill and there at the top was a gateway; and here I had to stop to see that rich and beautiful countryside with the evening light slanting across the meadows and the cornfields, looking like Traherne's vision, 'The corn was orient and immortal wheat, which never should be reaped, nor was ever sown. I thought it had stood from everlasting to everlasting.'

May I not share with Traherne his vision of felicity? May I not say with him, 'When I came into the country, and being seated among silent trees, and meads and hills, had all my time in mine own hands, I resolved to spend it all, whatever it cost me, in search of happiness, and to satiate that burning thirst which nature had enkindled in me from my youth.'

I have written as if all days were fine; but indeed some of the walks that I enjoyed most were in wet weather. In a soft summer rain under a gentle cloudy sky, the woods and meadows seemed as lovely to me as when the sun shone. I cannot forget the pleasure of walking in the lanes or in the woods in the rain, seeing silver drops hanging from the twigs and the trunks of the trees shining with wet, being conscious that every growing thing appeared to lift itself up, to expand on a wet day after a time of drought.

On Sundays we walked to and from church. It was uphill most of the way there, so of course the return journey was easier. We usually went by the road, where, from a gateway in the estate wall, I have seen the millpond where I fished for perch a brilliant sparkling blue, like blue diamonds, dancing in the morning light beneath a fresh breeze. It seemed to call to me with the reminder that it would be Monday tomorrow, though I liked Sunday. We went to church as a matter of course and there we heard, and I feel sure absorbed, the beauty of the Authorized Version of the Bible and the 1662 prayerbook. I remember one summer Sunday when there was a thunderstorm the Rector read some verses of Psalm Twenty Nine and likened the rolling of the thunder to the splendid words.

'The voice of the Lord breaketh the cedar-trees', 'The voice of the Lord maketh the hinds to bring forth young, and discovereth the thick bushes.' I was a small boy, yet that memory has stayed with me all my life.

I have already quoted Trevelyan and I will venture to do so again. Speaking of all kinds of people at the time of Izaak Walton, he writes, 'All were subject to the wholesome influence of that time and landscape. Their language was the crisp pure English from which the translators of the Bible drew their style.' It may seem that there was a great distance between the time of Izaak Walton and Bunyan and the time of which I am writing; but I do not think the gap between the sixteenth century and the time when I was young was as great, in quiet country places at all events, as the gap between that time and this, when noise, speed and mass production have largely destroyed a sense of tradition.

I have already written of the Biblical turn of speech which was a common everyday occurrence. If anyone doubts this then let them read the books and the poems of Thomas Hardy or the plays of Eden Philpots. The language of the Bible is potent in these works.

In those days it was common in country churches when there was no choir to hear the psalms read, one verse by the Rector, one by the congregation. I think I never heard that beautiful language more perfectly than on these occasions, but I believe what made it so memorable was that I heard, what I may call, two versions, each in its way of a high order.

First came the Rector, with old-fashioned cultivated diction, clear and precise.

RECTOR: 'The river of God is full of water: thou preparest their corn, for so thou providest for the earth.'
CONGREGATION: 'Thou waterest the furrows, thou sendest rain into the little valleys thereof: thou makest it soft with the drops of rain and blessest the increase of it.'

The contrast between the two, the one clear and cultivated, the other a wonderful, rich, burring sound, did, I believe, achieve an unforgettable whole. Not only was the language so fine, and so easily understood and felt by the people, but the imagery was an essential part of their lives.

'Thou preparest their corn — .' 'Thou waterest the furrows'. 'Thou makest it soft with the drops of rain'. These things were the very substance of their everyday life and their lives depended upon such things, they were their daily preoccupation.

Sometimes we walked to church across the fields. I think walking to church is quite the nicest way of getting there, with the possible exception of driving in a pony trap. To approach the church by a path that meanders among fields and meadows, perhaps through a stretch of woodland, puts one into precisely the right state of mind; all the way one can hear the bells, a sound which seems to impregnate the very air, the sunshine itself, with a feeling of Sunday. Meadows never look so green and still, corn so golden, cows so contented, as they do on a fine Sunday morning. However beautiful a town church may be, it lacks a quality which our old village churches possess. It is as though in a physical as well as in a spiritual sense the church and churchyard, with the sound of bells on Sunday and the chiming of the clock during the week, form a kind of focal point in a village. Even those who never go inside it are conscious of it. It seems to draw all towards it and to radiate a force, an influence, to the farthest corner.

As we crossed the cornfields when the corn was fully grown, we walked between walls which were first green and then, as harvest approached, gold. I know that wheat is grown with a shorter straw now to avoid laying, but it seems to me, looking back, that the walls of the wheat were as high as my head so that I looked into a maze of corn stalks, a miniature forest. The last stage of the field path crossed a meadow and came out where two lanes met. Here we were at the top of the hill, and we stopped for a moment to look back at the view to a gleam of sea in the distance. I was told that the great landscape painter, Turner, had painted this view, but in the light of more recent knowledge I think this story is probably in the same category as those of the beds in which Queen Elizabeth has slept.

After the last stile we came to a grassy bank beside the lane, where the village lads congregated on a Sunday morning, all in

blue serge suits, often with a rose or some flower in their
buttonholes, and with large caps worn over one ear. Blue serge
was common then for Sunday suits, which had one peculiarity;
a Sunday suit could never become a working suit but was put
away for Sundays and holidays. I always disliked seeing the
country people in their best clothes; I was used to seeing them
during the week in their working clothes. That was how I
knew and liked them. In Sunday clothes, although the girls
could look very pretty, the boys and men seemed uneasy and
unfamiliar.

We were very fortunate in that we were free to go almost
anywhere, including the estate within the park walls where the
ponds were in which we fished or bathed. One of the commonest sights when we wandered inside the park walls was
the large number of pheasants, which were reared by the
gamekeeper. The little, drab hen birds always seemed to me
like quiet, inoffensive women who knew their place. Not so the
splendid cock birds with their gorgeous green and red heads,
white wattles and strutting walk. Game birds were to be seen
everywhere, not only in the woods but on the banks of the lanes.
An unmistakable sound was the sudden crowing of the cocks,
which I cannot hear now without remembering those woods
and lanes. If one put up a pheasant from the undergrowth the
sudden whirr of its wings, its rocketing flight and its startled,
loud ringing cry were unforgettable. Another sight which was
common then was the numbers of rabbits playing in the
meadows by the woods on a summer evening before one had
heard of myxomatosis. I am well aware of the harm done to
crops and the bark of young trees by rabbits, but I am
remembering them as a small boy would.

From the wall of the churchyard, where the door for the
Squire's family was, an earth road ran to a gate opening into the
lane and we often walked that way. The road ran for a distance
of a mile or more through an avenue of tall old lime trees in
which there were many holes where jackdaws, magpies, owls
and woodpeckers roosted. When I think of this lane it is always
to the accompaniment of the cawing of rooks, the high sharp
'Chack! Chack!' of the jackdaws and the rattle of the
woodpeckers, or the 'Twite! Twite!' of nuthatches. A kind of

under-sound was the 'Chee! Chee! Chee!' of families of tits searching for grubs.

Some of our walks were quite long. One day I had a notice that my white kid which I had bought had arrived by train at the little market town five miles away. My sister and I borrowed a little cart made of a box on old pram wheels and walked to the station to fetch it. It was a lovely road, much of it being through woods, and we had often walked it, but it was five miles each way and quite a long distance pushing the little cart for a small boy and girl.

Another of our longer walks which meant a day out for the family was to an old and, to me, romantic house standing beside a lake in an extensive park: the lake was full of golden carp. There was a lodge near by where we often persuaded the lodge-keeper's wife to make us some tea. The old, weathered, red brick of the house and of a small bridge from where we could watch the carp, together with the rather neglected garden and many old trees, gave the place something of the atmosphere of a fairy story.

Shops and Shopping

I SUPPOSE one of the greatest changes since I was small has been the change in shops and shopping. The growth of the multiple store and the supermarket, and of advertising on television, has completely altered the situation. In villages even the old village shop, which I have already attempted to describe as I remember it, has been increasingly replaced by a smaller version of the 'self-service store'.

One of the nicest of these vanished shops was the saddler and harness-maker. As you entered one I knew well there was a wooden counter on the right, stretching from the window back into the shop, which was also a workshop. In the window, behind the counter, hanging from beams and from trees on the walls, were saddles, bridles, bits of all sorts, head collars, enormous collars for draught horses, girths, stirrup irons, sets of reins, traces, every kind of harness for riding, for light horses and for heavy ones. There were halters made of rope and canvas webbing, tools for picking stones from a horse's hoof, horse blankets and saddle pads, tins of neatsfoot oil and saddle soap, sponges and polishing cloths and dandy brushes, curry combs, bottles of liniment and Stockholm tar for coughs — every conceivable thing that you could need for horses. In addition there were leather straps, dog collars and leads, riding crops, leather trunks and all kinds of leather goods. Two brothers kept the shop and when you entered they would both be at work in the back of the shop. One would come forward to attend to you and the other would go on with his stitching, punching and cutting.

There was often a half-made saddle on a wooden horse, an example of the skill and craftsmanship of such workmen, and the whole shop was permeated with the smell of leather, harness oil and beeswax.

I remember one day, before the Second World War, when I was driving a pony trap through Alcester. I had broken a piece of harness and I stopped at the saddler's, long since gone, to get it repaired. It was a pleasant experience. The saddler was an elderly man, and he came out with his shirt sleeves rolled up and wearing a canvas apron. As he mended the harness for me he talked of people and places in the neighbourhood, looked at the pony and asked me where I was bound for. Although there were still quite a lot of horses and traps to be seen in quieter parts I think we already had a sense of not belonging to the present day; of being survivors of a passing fraternity.

There was often a smithy in little towns, for many people came from the country round about on market day in traps, gigs and carts or on horseback. There was plenty of bustle and noise, but it was a pleasant, crowded scene and I had a sense as I looked around that all those ruddy faced, weather-beaten folk came from villages and remote farmsteads in the countryside round about. Market day was a holiday for the women, who liked to meet and have a cup of tea, and for the children, as well as for farmers and farm-workers.

These weekly, market day gatherings are among my most pleasant memories. The crowds were often shabby and rough but the shabbiness was not that of the town. Their clothes were weatherworn, even the market day hats showed signs of exposure to wind and rain in open traps and carts; their boots were thick and strong; but it was a pleasant roughness which, with their weather-beaten faces and their burring, rounded speech, conjured up a life of farmyards and farm kitchens, of labour in fields and gardens, and all the round of rural life. Outside the inn, where the farmers gathered, were men and boys with battered mackintoshes, boots and gaiters, sticks and staves and dogs, their talk being of weather, cattle and sheep; of hay and corn and roots and prices. I have never been happier nor felt more at home than among such folk and in such an atmosphere.

The market itself was a hive of activity with its stalls and its cheap-jacks. There was nearly always a man selling pots or the like who was a well-known character, with a fund of back-chat and banter echoed by bursts of laughter from the crowd. There was no attempt at anything artistic with fancy prices. The crocks and pots and other ware were bought by people who were going to use them. One could buy wonderful earthenware bowls, jugs, dishes and crocks for laying down eggs or runner beans in salt, or for bread; wide shallow pans for milk, which would stand on stone slabs in the dairy for the cream to settle, the cream being skimmed off with flat skimmers; and many other things which had the curious, simple beauty without self-consciousness peculiar to such things. So much at that time had a kind of unconscious beauty, a quality that seemed a part of its nature and nothing to do with artists or craft workers.

A shop which I always liked was the ironmonger's. Here was the same kind of variety as in the saddler's. There were scythes, sickles and billhooks, garden tools, staels to fit anything, buckets, real ones not plastic; bunches of rabbit snares, mole traps, fishing tackle, stable lanterns of the large sort that one cannot get now, and square lanterns for burning candles; traps for rats and mice, both break-back ones and the cage type, which I have not seen for a long time. There were many kinds of oil lamps: standing lamps with one or two burners for the table; lamps with reflectors for hanging on the wall; carrying lamps of many sizes; candlesticks, and a great variety of lamp glasses, chimneys and shades, for it was rare for any farm or country house or cottage to have any other form of lighting.

I have seen plays on television which have reproduced the interiors of houses and cottages of that time remarkably well; but over and over again I have noticed curious faults in the type of oil lamps used and in their handling. I lived with oil lamps for a good many years, and as I cleaned them and cared for them I have had a good deal of experience. Often in such productions I have seen characters light the lamps in entirely the wrong way. They turn up the wicks far too high, so that when the glass chimney is put on the flames are much too large. Not only is there a danger that the glass will crack, but the lamps will smoke — as indeed they do — and the glass will be blackened. The wicks should be lit turned down as low as they will burn and only turned up gradually until the glass chimney grows warm.

But there is another fault which is very common. We used different kinds of lamps for different purposes. There were wall lamps made to hang on a nail on a wall, with a flat back and a mirror to reflect the light into the room; and there were standing lamps of various kinds, made to stand on a table or a secure base. These might have one or two wicks, and usually had a glass chimney with either a round globe or a shade. The fault which I have noticed so often is that someone will pick up a table lamp and carry it to a door or window, if a visitor arrives, or round a room. This is quite wrong and no one who was used to lamps would do this – the flames would immediately flare up and the glass become blackened with smoke or break in the draught. I have often seen actors in a period play carrying a lamp in this way, tilting it out of the straight. We would never carry a table lamp – we had small carrying lamps, usually with a broad base, a short, squat, chimney and a handle at the side. One of the commonest faults, even with a hurricane lantern, is that the wick is turned up too high too soon; and this is very noticeable if one has been used to lamps.

The grocer's and sweet shops were a larger addition of the village shop, where things were sold by weight and pre-packaged goods were rare. The sweet shops were full of tall glass jars of sweets, and the grocer's looked very gay, especially at Christmas when the windows were full of candied orange and lemon peel pushed up against the glass of the shop front. One of the greatest changes is at the chemists', which usually had their windows full of enormous bottles with spiky tops, full of bright red, green, blue and orange liquid which I suppose was coloured water.

One kind of shop which has completely disappeared is the old-fashioned toy shop. They were marvellous places which sold toys of a kind which have vanished with the shops. There were wax dolls with golden hair and bright blue eyes which opened and shut. If you left them in the sun the wax would melt and the eyes would stick, usually shut, as the doll lying on the ground was 'asleep'. There were stuffed toys, both animals and little men, which we called brownies. I had one stuffed with broken cork. He had a red cap and a rosy face. He was known as 'Sprity', and he became almost a family mascot. Alas, he became old and developed a leak so that the cork ran out and he collapsed like a pricked balloon. I was really stricken by his loss and although I was given another, a green one, he was never the same as Sprity.

There were a great many gaily painted wooden toys, but, alas, many of these bore the legend 'Made in Germany' and fell into disfavour. I had a wonderful wagon with two dapple-grey horses. It was full of barrels which you could unload, and the horses could be unharnessed. And there were Jack-in-the-boxes and gaudy humming tops. Two toys that I have not seen for many years are Dutch dolls made of wood, with jointed limbs and round heads with black hair painted on the head with a parting in the middle, and a round blob of red on each cheek; and golliwogs, real ones with black faces and with round, white-ringed eyes, red mouths and a mass of black golliwog hair, with blue jackets and red waistcoats, brass buttons and red trousers. I regarded these with a mixture of pleasure and fear. I liked them in the daytime but I remember waking once at night, when I was a very small boy, and seeing one propped up against the bed-post at the bottom of my bed. Perhaps it was that bright red smile and those white-ringed eyes in the light of a candle, but I howled the place down until grown-ups came rushing in. All attempts to reassure me failed, and golly was banished.

One thing I longed to have – a rocking horse. A splendid large one, a dapple-grey with flaring red nostrils and flying back mane and tail, stood in a passage when I was taken to see my grandmother in a tall and, to me, rather sinister, shadowy house, with dark panelled passages and stairways, where my grandmother and an aunt lived in faded and rather creepy splendour. I used to ride it while my mother visited my grandmother. But such things were beyond us and only to be found in the nurseries of rich children. I believe this one had belonged to my mother and her brothers and sister when they were children and had lived in rather grander style.

One of the most fascinating shops to me, when I was very small, was the draper's. These shops with their piled-up bales of coloured materials and their mahogany counters had a curious, cosy fug and a smell that was their own; but the thing that fascinated me was the overhead railway through which one paid one's money. The shop assistant took the money, wrapped it in the bill and then unscrewed the top of a canister. When the money and the bill were placed inside, the canister was put into a kind of catapult. The assistant pulled a handle and let go and the canister shot off at a tremendous rate along wires high above the shoppers. It whizzed along with a humming noise until it came to a set of points, as a train might, when with a click it changed course. It might do this several times before it disappeared. When it had disappeared into the bowels of the shop, I waited with fascinated watchfulness until the wire began to hum and the flying canister appeared once again in the distance, and came racing back at great speed to drop with a crash into a wire basket, form where the shop-assistant retrieved it and unscrewed the top to let the receipted bill and one's change fall out. The fascination of this never failed and I longed to have such an aerial railway of my own so that I could transmit messages to my friends.

One could continue indefinitely in this vein, but I suppose the real loss is a human one. It was all so much simpler, slower, to me happier.

Books

WHEN I look back and realize how much reading, and being read to, mattered to us all from our earliest days, I am thankful that I was born into a family where such things were encouraged. It was not so in all families. I knew of some in which reading was looked upon with disfavour, as a form of idleness. But we were brought up to believe that 'a good book is the life-blood of a master spirit'. I was fortunate in this as in so many things, for my pleasures lay around me. By modern standards we had practically no pocket money and entertainments were rare; but our lives, based as they were upon a secure and happy home life, were full of contentment.

Among my greatest pleasure was reading: in winter by the fire; in summer in some favourite spot out of doors or in a sheltered place according to the weather. I was something of a connoisseur of 'places' for reading, for it has always been a matter of importance to me to read a book in the right atmosphere. I have been trying to remember some of the books which I read, but as the earliest were fifty or sixty years ago, or more, my memory may be hazy or inaccurate.

Books, in those early years, were divided for me into two main kinds: books which one read on Sunday and books which belonged to the rest of the week. The idea of there being a difference between weekday books and Sunday books may seem odd to many people today. I fancy it would evoke expressions of scorn among many who regard themselves as being enlightened. It is true that my father was something of a

Sabbatrian, but I can assure any who feel critical of such ideas that the result, as far as I was concerned, was not to make me believe that Sunday books were 'good' and weekday books 'wicked'. I was used to regarding Sunday as different from any other day. We did not play games on Sunday, we went to church: but whatever theorists today may think I liked Sunday and thought of it as a special day.

I will write about Sunday books first. Some of those which we read or which were read to us, for 'reading aloud' especially on Sunday evenings was common then, would no doubt strike me as being mawkish now; but many gave me great pleasure. I was not, of course, a Victorian, but a number of books of this kind had a character which was inherited from that time, or were actually Victorian books given to us by friends or relatives who had had them as children. The older ones were often bound in heavy boards with gilt lettering, and had the curious black and white illustrations of that time.

One which I remember, indeed I still have the actual copy that I read as a small boy, was Mrs Gatty's *Parables from Nature*. I loved it, morals and all. This very copy lies on the table as I write. Inside is written in careful copper-plate writing, 'Percy Gaster from Clara, 1892'. These were my father and my aunt. My father was born in 1868, so he was twenty-four when my aunt gave him this book. It is bound in very faded green cloth boards, which I believe were called 'limp boards'. Mrs Gatty's daughter, Juliana Horatia Ewing, has written a memoir of her mother at the beginning of the book. It has the curious, to me sometimes rather creepy, illustrations of which I have written and the illustrators are listed as being P. H. Calderon, W. Holman Hunt, Otto Speckter, G. H. Thomas, John Tenniel, and others. It was published by George Bell & Sons, London, York Street, Covent Garden in 1891. As it is a very good example of a 'Sunday book' I will spend a little time on it.

Every story is prefaced by a quotation from scripture. I will give the titles and quotations of one or two. The first is called, 'A Lesson of Faith', and the quotation is, 'If a man die, shall he live *again*? All the days of my appointed time will I wait, till my change come'. Job 14:14.

The opening words are,

'Let me hire you as a nurse for my poor children', said a Butterfly to a quiet Caterpillar, who was strolling along a cabbage leaf in her odd, lumbering way. 'See these little eggs', continued the Butterfly; 'I don't know how long it will be before they come to life, and I feel very sick and poorly, and if I should die, who will take care of my baby butterflies when I am gone?'

Then comes, 'The Unknown Land'. 'But now they desire a better country.' Hebrews 11:16. This chapter opens, 'It mattered not to the Sedge Warbler whether it were night or day!' Another chapter is called, 'Knowledge not the Limit of Belief', and its quotation is, 'Canst thou by searching find out God?' Job 11:7.

Other titles were 'The Circle of Blessing', 'Active and Passive', 'Daily Bread', 'Red Snow', 'Inferior Animals', 'Waiting', 'Gifts', and so on.

But the one that I loved best of all and that still has a curious fascination for me is, 'The Light of Truth'. There are two intriguing pictures to this: one is of a girl knee-deep in a bog and surrounded by rushes; the other of a man on a horse and a boy on a pony apparently approaching the same bog. They are in a strange, dark landscape with streaks of light along the horizon, and they are seen as dark shapes against the lowering sky. Indeed these are both examples of the eerie illustrations which were so often a feature of such books. But the weirdest, and to me the most fascinating thing in both pictures is the 'Will-o-the-Wisp' which is hovering above the marsh. I remember asking my mother what it was and, on being told, I longed to see one. The opening words are, '"Detestable Phantom!" cried the traveller, as his horse sank with him into the morass. "To what a miserable end have you lured me by your treacherous light!"'

I used to look at these two pictures over and over again. I found something of the same fascination in the illustrations to *The Back of the North Wind* by George MacDonald and, above all, in the illustrations to *Oliver Twist* by Cruikshank, especially the picture of Fagin in his condemned cell.

Mrs Juliana Horatia Ewing was another Sunday favourite of ours. I remember my mother reading to us *Jan of the Windmill* and *Jackanapes* by the fire. In those days ladies wore many voluminous skirts and petticoats and, as so many ladies did, my mother would turn her skirt back to avoid its being scorched: I liked to sit on the hearthrug leaning against her, and I can still smell the hot fire on her petticoat for she loved to sit close to the warmth.

I regard these and others of the same kind as books of a high quality; but there were others which did not approach their standard. Many of these came under the heading, 'Sunday School Prize', and were often of a moral and didactic nature; but even so some of them still have nostalgic associations for me. They were often stories of family life with titles like *The Mad Ruthvens* (who were tamed by a saintly invalid cousin), *Winning the Victory*, and so on. There were many more of which the memory is faint, but they had certain things in common: one of these was their moral tone; then they abounded in death-bed scenes, illnesses or injuries which had been incurred by disobedience, with repentance following after a suitable time on a sick-bed; or misunderstandings, when virtuous children were wrongly blamed for evil deeds perpetrated by wicked children, and other such things. My younger sister was very tender-hearted and when such events occurred, if the book was being read to us, she would weep and say, 'Pass over that part!'

I remember a tale of a small girl who lived by a churchyard. Her chief recreation was throwing flowers which she had picked into newly dug graves, and there was a chapter called, I think, 'The Flower Fadeth', in which she came to an early end and converted several hardened sinners, including the horny-handed grave-digger.

But they were by no means all like that. I have already mentioned the works of Mrs Ewing. Others which I recall were *Little Lord Fauntleroy*, *Christy's Old Organ*, *A Peep behind the Scenes*, *Uncle Tom's Cabin*, and the works of Amy Le Feuvre, *Odd*, *Odd made Even*, *Laddie's Choice*, *A Little Maid*. I also took great pleasure in reading of the exploits of missionaries, such as *Mackay of Uganda*, *David Livingstone*, *Mary Slessor of Calabar*, and indeed they still seem to me to have been remarkable people.

But of course there were many more weekday books; indeed I read so many that I cannot possibly remember them. We were often given books at Christmas, and among early presents were *Blackie's Annual* and *Bran Pie*. I had no idea what *Annual* meant, or that there were other volumes; it was simply a book we always called *Blackie's Anniall*. *Bran Pie* gave me great pleasure when I was very small. It was a fat, green book with gold lettering on the cover. Inside were many stories which I read over and over again, and some pictures that I remember very clearly. One was of two elves flying through the air on bumble-bees, and charging each other with spears made of grass stalks. Another was of a prince with a drawn sword, in a wood full of weird trees with faces and long, knotty branch-arms and spiky fingers plucking at him. I think it must have been drawn by Arthur Rackham. There was a curious story about a girl called Sylvia, who was queen of the rabbits and a boy called William Henry Gunnersbury. One picture showed Sylvia with thousands of rabbits; a full moon cast a weird light over the scene, which created in me a mixture of pleasure and fear.

Many early books were distinctly sinister. When I was ten or twelve I was given a box of books which had belonged to a man I knew when he was a boy. One had an extraordinarily creepy story in it, called 'The Dead Usher'. Another was a collection of Sherlock Holmes stories. I remember a winter evening when I read 'The Five Dried Orange Pips' to my sisters. It may seem incredible but we were so frightened when I finished that we put the book on the fire.

A book which I loved very much was *Tales from the Norse*. I never liked the classic legends but I delighted in these (a curious portent when one remembers that, many years later, I married a Scandinavian!) This was one of the books in which I lived. It was a large volume with gothic-looking line pictures of giants, trolls and dark forests. The stories I particularly remember were 'East o' the Sun and West o' the Moon', 'The Princess on the Glass Hill', 'Shortshanks', 'The Blue Belt', 'Dapplegrim'. The incidents that fascinated me in 'The Princess on the Glass Hill' were the times when 'Boots' kept a vigil to see what was eating their hay in the outlying field on the hillside. In his three vigils he acquired three splendid horses, each with a suit of armour, a saddle and a bridle. The first were all of copper, the second of silver and the third of gold. When I came to know Sweden, I was fascinated to find little meadows away in the forest surrounded by dark trees, and with buildings made of pine logs just like those in which Boots kept his vigil. There was another story in which a farmer grazed his cow on the roof of the farmhouse, which I never could understand until I saw red wooden farmhouses and barns roofed with turves which grew a fine crop of grass.

'Shortshanks' had a little tiny ship which he could carry in his pocket. When he wanted to use it he laid it on the ground, and put first one foot then the other into it and it grew bigger and bigger until he could sail in it. Then he would say, 'Off and away, over fresh water and salt water, over high hills and deep dales and don't stop till you come to the King's palace,' or wherever he wanted to go. I longed to have such a ship, to fight many-headed ogres and come back with a load of gold and silver rings as large as hoops. The classic tales of rather anaemic gods and goddesses seemed poor stuff after trolls and ogres, magic ships, belts and splendid horses, gold and silver and dark mysterious forests.

Among my favourites as I grew older were the stories by R. M. Ballantyne, W. H. Kingston, and especially George Manville Fenn – the one I liked best by him was *Dick of the Fens*. This was full of duck shooting and snaring, fishing, leaping across stretches of water with long poles, and of Dick himself, a genuine antiprogressive type who was ready to do anything to prevent the fens from being 'dree-erned'. I loved all such books about hunters, trappers and poachers, whether in England or in the forests, lakes and the frozen wastes of Canada or the Arctic – books about icebergs, kayaks, polar bears, seals and Eskimos; about blubber and pemmican, fur traders, bad men and Indians.

Among my greatest favourites was a book called *On the Banks of the Amazon* by Ballantyne. When I read this, as I did over and over again, I lived in a world of jungles and dug-out canoes, of blow-pipes, and spider-monkeys and lianes; of floating islands, tree-houses, strange wild fruits and flowers, and hot nights in tropical forests full of strange smells and whooping, howling and roaring animals. An enchanted world.

Then there were *Robinson Crusoe*, *The Swiss Family Robinson*, *Masterman Ready*, *Ungava*, *The Man Eaters of the Tsavo*, and *The Dog Crusoe*, a tale of prairies, mustangs, vast herds of wild buffalo and hunters who could shoot a piece of grass out of your mouth without touching you.

There was *The Princess and Curdie*, *The Princess and the Goblins*, *Sylvie and Bruno* by Lewis Carroll, with the songs of the mad gardener,

> He thought he saw a polar bear
> Which skated on the ice.
> He looked again and saw it was
> A pudding made of rice.
> 'If one might have plum cake', he said
> 'I'd rather have a slice.'

When I came to read *Sylvie and Bruno* again I found it intolerably mawkish.

I might go on and on: to the immortal classic, *The Secret Garden*; to Dickens and Thackeray, Scott and R. L. Stevenson, *The Jungle Books* and *Puck of Pook's Hill* and *Rewards and Fairies*; to Captain Marryat, *The Hunchback of Notre Dame* and Jules Verne, and heaven knows what else.

I never really liked school stories, with the exception of *Tom Brown's School Days*, and there was one kind of school story to which I took great exception. These were written by women who must have had the oddest ideas about what went on in boys' schools. They were written in an excessively hearty, jolly way, the boys constantly addressing each other with 'Chaps', 'I say chaps', or perhaps 'You fellows', and they were always having 'topping' or 'ripping' times. They reminded me of a type of woman whom I found extremely embarrassing, who would say to me at a tea-party, 'Come and sit by me! I understand boys!' They would thump me on the back and tell me in very loud voices, 'We are having a spiffing time, aren't we!' It must have been rather obvious that I was not.

The Nature of English
Landscape Painting

I AM not attempting to write a book on painting, but since I am
a painter and since I have already written of the nature of the
English countryside, perhaps I may venture a few remarks on
English landscape painting. It is not easy to compress all that I
would like to say into one short essay, so I run the risk of
appearing to express myself in an arbitrary manner, but I will
take that risk in the hope that I can convey part of what I feel so
strongly.

I have often felt that we do not realize the extent to which
geographical position and climate affect the temper and the
works of art produced by any nation. I think this is particularly
important in considering English landscape painting. England
is, or was during our most productive and most characteristic
period, an island; and if we add to this our climate and our
landscape, both of which are mild and almost totally devoid of
excess, I think we have discovered a conditioning force of the
greatest importance.

Some years ago Nikolaus Pevsner delivered an admirable
series of Reith Lectures entitled 'The Englishness of English
Art'. It is always interesting to hear the comments of someone
who has an outside view; and Pevsner said that, coming as he
did as a foreigner to England, having been reared in the atmosphere of Austrian Baroque, what stood out in England was a
kind of plainness, an absence of rhetoric or extravagance; and
he added that however much a man may be himself, he is also

determined by the age in which he lives and the country to which he belongs.

In his book *Art and Society* Herbert Read wrote (before Pevsner's lectures),

> Landscape painting is very typical of the English tradition, but no one has ever given a good definition of this tradition and I could wish some foreigner would do it for us.

> It is *inconceivable* that Gainsborough and Constable could be anything but Englishmen, and yet it is very difficult to say what quality they have in common which makes them so inalienably English. It concerns, perhaps, their attitude towards nature, and perhaps a key to this attitude can be found in another Art, in English poetry. The secret is in Wordsworth's counsel, 'Let nature be your teacher', as well as in Constable's phrase, 'The pure apprehension of natural fact'. It is an attitude of *trust* in nature – an attitude far removed from the aggressive 'Sachlichkeit' of German Art and the sardonic 'Reálisme' of French Art. The passivity of the artist is essential. You cannot take nature by storm. This is partly the secret of the English tradition. There is also a quality which is perhaps not so creditable. Again it is not easy to define exactly, but I think it is an outcome of the English love of comfort. The English 'nature' is purely apprehended, but it is not thickly populated. What I mean to imply is that for the English nature is in some sense a refuge from life.

I have quoted this in full because it expresses so admirably, and so much better than I could myself, what I feel to be true. There is only one word that I would alter, and that is the word 'comfort', although I think I understand what Read means, I feel the word 'security' is a little less self-indulgent.

'The English "nature" is purely apprehended but it is not thickly populated' – this sentence strikes me as particularly perceptive. It may seem hard to say this, but the peculiar beauty of England is so small and so frail that it cannot be invaded without being destroyed.

I have already written on the nature of the English landscape which nurtured this art, but I cannot pass on without one further reflection. There is no doubt that the great body of the best and most essentially English work in landscape was produced in the eighteenth and nineteenth centuries. This is not to say that nothing good has been produced since, but it is true if one is thinking in general terms; and one might argue that the greatest landscape painting was produced when the English countryside was in its most beautiful and undefiled state. Much which has been done since may be considered 'interesting', but if you destroy that frail and special beauty you destroy the inspiration.

I cannot pass on without one more quotation, from Pevsner. Commenting on the fact that the bulk of English painting in the eighteenth and nineteenth centuries was landscape and portraiture he says, 'The reason that suggests itself is . . . that Renaissance and Baroque Art being Arts which glorify the human body and the heroic action did not appeal to the English. They neither believed in self-display nor in the grand manner of operatic ensemble.' He goes on to say, 'What led the English primarily to portrait and landscape as their chief outlet in painting is, to put it positively – faith in the observation of the particular rather than in sweeping generalities – *The observant eye* has been stressed time and again in English philosophy.' He writes of this 'observant eye' in painting being found in the marginal grotesques of English mediaeval manuscripts, through the enchanting 'genre' scenes on bosses and corbels, misericords and bench-ends in English architecture to Hogarth, English caricature and Victorian narrative painting and the pre-Raphaelites.

What strengthens my belief in all that I have tried to say is the close similarities to be found in English literature. The writings of Izaak Walton, Gilbert White, Richard Jeffries, John Clare, Wordsworth, Parson Woodeford, Kilvert, Edward Thomas, and many others are almost the exact parallel of true English landscape painting. One more influence I feel has had the greatest importance: puritanism. There can be no doubt that this is one of the most persistent qualities in the English character; indeed this fact is often emphasized by reactions away from puritanism, which frequently have a desperate and unnatural quality about them. Puritanism in this country has been of two kinds; positive and negative. In the seventeenth century puritanism in England had about it a fiery quality; one could say that it was so negative as to be positive. In the eighteenth century the atmosphere was cooled by rationalism and humanism; but by the nineteenth century puritanism was debased into philistinism and enduring British if not English quality; and morality became propriety. Negative puritanism is arrogant, bigoted and destructive, but positive puritanism has been the very soil in which our greatest productions in painting, literature and architecture have been rooted and grounded.

I think one may say that English landscape painting of the eighteenth and nineteenth centuries has two main strands. The first is composed of outstanding individual painters, men like Richard Wilson, John Crome, Gainsborough, Stubbs, Girtin, Constable, and some modern of whom I will write later. But there is also a second strand which we might call the folk art of English landscape. This embraces the best of the water-colourists from Paul Sandby onwards to such figures as John Sell Cotman, Francis Towne, David Cox, Prout, De Wint and many more. I think I would place Cotman and Francis Towne rather higher than this but I am speaking in generalities.

Ruskin has written of the minor English landscape painters in what I regard as an immortal passage, 'They were, themselves, a kind of contemplative cattle, and flock of the field, who merely liked being out of doors and brought as much painted fresh air as they could back into the house with them.' This is a wonderful description of a group of painters who were as delightfully English as the landscape itself, and as essential a part, in their small way, as the greatest.

It may seem odd that I have not even mentioned Turner. This is because he is in some ways, especially in his later work, the most un-English and exotic painter whom we have produced. For one thing his work almost entirely lacks an essential English ingredient – *Genius Loci*.

My belief that Constable is unquestionably the greatest painter of the essentially English landscape makes me feel that I must say a little more about him, for I believe he is a painter whose true nature has often been misunderstood. A great many people believe him to be the greatest of English landscape painters because of his realism, but this word is often used in its most trivial sense. The fact that he was much more than a realist in this sense of the word is proved by his own remarks about the work of another painter named Lee. 'I did not think his things were quite so bad. They pretend to nothing but *imitation of nature* but that is of the coldest and meanest kind. All is utterly heartless.'

Constable was the greatest painter of the English landscape because his best work conveys the very heart and essence of that landscape. Both the sketch and the final canvas of *The Leaping Horse*, which I believe to be the most complete of his major works, both in the technical and in the emotional sense, have a quality far beyond mere realism; they show an understanding of the essential England which makes them into major works of art.

If I were asked to recommend two pieces of writing which show the greatest penetration and understanding of what is most durable in Constable's work, I should choose the essay on Constable in Roger Fry's *Notes on English Painting*, and the remarks on his work in that remarkable book, *Landscape into Art* by Kenneth Clark.

I will quote Clark first.

> In his greatest work naturalism is raised to a higher mode by his belief that since nature was the clearest revelation of God's will, the painting of landscape, conceived in the spirit of humble truth, could be a means of conveying moral ideas — Wordsworth and Constable both believed that there was something, in trees, flowers, meadows and mountains which was so full of the divine that if it were contemplated with sufficient devotion it would reveal a moral and spiritual quality of its own — both believed that in humble themes 'the passions of men are incorporated with the beautiful and permanent forms of nature'.

The last words are, of course, quoted from Wordsworth. This is a great deal more than realism, for one cannot entertain such ideas unless one believes in a divine purpose behind nature.

Roger Fry, in the essay which I have mentioned, dwells on another, and equally important aspect of Constable's work. In a very fine analysis of what is perhaps the finest of the small paintings, *Malvernhall* in the National Gallery, Fry claims that Constable is an example of the true contemplative in painting and I must quote one passage:

> Certain *visual experiences* compel them [great artists] to this detached contemplative attitude, and the work of art comes to us as the expression of that newly discovered significance. When we come to Constable we shall see that his work is full of such discoveries of significant moments in his *visual* life.

> Within his range he has never been surpassed or even equalled. Nearly every one of his small studies is a discovery – a discovery of some moment when the tones and colours reveal themselves as suddenly brought together in a new and altogether unexpected harmony.

One does not have to be a painter to realize that this is much more than the commonly accepted idea of realism.

There is one point in connection with the painting of nature and of current ideas on art which disturbs me. When I was visiting an exhibition I was invited to admire a water-colour of a cock 'becoming a bunch of flowers'. I believe this is to be an example of a pseudo-philosophy, a false profundity, which is very common in art today. There is a passage in Ruskin which makes my point clearly. Writing on three classes of perception, he says,

> There is first the man who perceives rightly, because he does not feel, and to whom the primrose is very accurately the primrose, because he does not love it. Then, secondly, the man who perceives wrongly, because he feels, and to whom the primrose is anything else than a primrose; a star, or a sun, or a fairy's shield, or a forsaken maiden. And then, lastly, there is the man who perceives rightly in spite of his feelings, and to whom the primrose is forever nothing else than itself – a little flower apprehended in the very plain and leafy fact of it, whatever and how many soever the associations and passions may be that crowd around it.

Kenneth Clark comments, 'To this class, as Ruskin says, belong poets of the highest order.'

I think it is not generally realized that there are two kinds of imagination in painting: that which imagines or creates forms which did not exist before; and that which perceives with creative intensity things which already exist, or, to quote Kenneth Clark once more, 'Facts become art through love, which unifies them and lifts them to a higher plane of reality.'

I cannot leave these brief notes on a fascinating subject without touching on one point which seems to me important. It is a curious fact that very few landscape painters have been countrymen. Perhaps it is not so curious, for a landscape painter may well come to the countryside with a sharpened awareness, a kind of hunger, springing from the very fact that he is a townsman. But when he is a countryman it gives his work a quality which makes it different from landscape; he is not so much a landscape painter as a country painter; by a country painter I mean a man whose whole life is based upon love of and knowledge of a true country life, which creates a conditioning force.

At random I can think of very few painters who are of this kind. To go back some way Pieter Brueghel is a splendid example. In his paintings, such as *The Seasons, Corn Harvest*, or *Hay-harvest*, he shows the intimate awareness of the man, and the painter, who knows the very nature of the seasons, of heat and cold, snow and ice and water and mud, and common rural activities seen realistically and with knowledge of their everyday effect on rural people. Rubens is a magnificent *landscape* painter but he can never achieve this intimacy with common things. His peasants are never so real as Brueghel's.

Gainsborough shows this intimacy in such early paintings as *Mr and Mrs Andrews* in their park, one of the most complete rural pictures to come out of English painting. Constable is a countryman; Turner is not. He is too grand, he grasps the force and drama of the elements but the *countryside* is not in his blood as it is in Constable's.

Coming to modern times I would single out two painters who have this special quality, John Nash and George Clausen. The curious thing about John Nash is that he and his brother, Paul

Nash, were both, I believe, born in Kensington. They had the land in their blood, for I understand that their forebears farmed in Suffolk; but while John reverts to that background, Paul does not. He is an urban and complex painter even when he paints landscape, while, in my opinion, no modern artist has shown a greater understanding of rural England than his brother, John.

I think few modern painters have affected me more than George Clausen; and here I must mention something which I feel to be a curious reflection on the temper of the times in which we live. I have found that even among those who show an intelligent and perceptive interest in landscape painting, the great majority have never seen or heard of the paintings of George Clausen. Even a writer for whom I have a considerable respect, Sir John Rothenstein, late director of the Tate Gallery, did not include him in his books on 'Modern English Painters'.

Recently when I was staying with a friend, I came on an old bound volume of *The Royal Academy Illustrated*. I could not see what year it was, but judging by the names of the painters I think it must have been early in this century. I turned the pages with a kind of fascination, and the one outstanding impression that I received from them was the extreme badness of the paintings. They were of a triviality and a sentimentality almost beyond description, particularly the landscapes, which lacked style or any redeeming feature; with one great exception, a small, and bad, reproduction of a barn interior by George Clausen.

I have already written of my affection for barns and I know of no other painter since the Flemish primitives, with the exception of Jean François Millet at his rural best (by which I do not mean *The Angelus*) who can paint a barn interior with such an intense understanding and such beautiful technique as George Clausen. No reproduction can really convey the quality of his technique or of his feeling for his medium.

He painted many barn interiors, and this was a good example. The great doors were open and the light flooded in, lighting up the floor and accentuating the dimness of the church-like interior with the beautiful massive timbers of the roof and the posts. Two men were at work, typical Clausen figures, shovelling a great heap of, I suppose, corn but the reproduction was small; the dim masses of sacks and piles of hay or straw were beautifully seen and felt against the light; in the wall of the barn was one of those little windows that I have tried to describe through which one saw a glimpse of sunlit countryside like a brilliant Flemish miniature.

No recent painter, not even John Nash, can convey to me the special beauty of the English farming countryside with greater intensity than Clausen. If one adds to the barns his September mornings, November mornings, paintings of frost and mist and summer sunrises, and to those his increasingly lyrical water-colours, the best of which belong to his latest period, then one has a painter who has celebrated not just the English landscape, but the English countryside as few have.

Christmas

ONE of the greatest joys of real country life, especially in a remote place far from the artificial pleasures and distractions of a town, is the passing of the seasons. When one's life is lived in such a place, not only each season but each month also has a character which makes it quite different from any other. Each time of year has its effect on the life and work of those whose lives are lived close to natural changes. I have always had a strong feeling for times and seasons, and believe that it would be very sad to live one's life so far removed from the seasons of the year and the changes in the weather as to be only half-aware of them or even to regard them as unavoidable nuisances.

As the summer drew towards its end one became aware of many such changes. From the going of the swallows one was daily more conscious of natural portents. The days became shorter, the winds cooler. Towards evening great flocks of starlings went over to their roosting place; one morning there came the 'Chutt! Chutt!' of a flock of fieldfares, and one could hear the cawing of rooks from the newly ploughed fields and perhaps on a still evening the weird cry of the vixen fox.

In the later autumn days, when the air was mild as milk and the sky the peculiar blue that goes with the gold of the stubbles, the air was filled with floating cobwebs, so fine as to be invisible until, catching a gleam from the sun, they shone like strands of silver. Low down in the hedge or on the stubble were cobwebs like hammocks, while higher up, stretched across a gateway or the twigs of a tree, were splendid spiders' webs, so beautiful in design and so perfectly placed that, when one saw them spangled with dew in the morning as the faint mists cleared, one felt there must be some consciousness, some absolute beauty behind them. In the warmth of the day the world seemed the expression of perfect peace and stillness, a world of blue and gold and silver, of ripe fruit and the drowsy hum of bees.

The air grew sharper with a chill in it and then one morning there was the first frost, silver and evanescent, vanishing with the early rays of the sun. As the leaves turned one heard a sound that is inseparable to me from that place and that time of year, the constant calling of pheasants from the woods. Soon there was a shooting party at the Hall, and the cries of the beaters and the sound of them thrashing the bushes with their sticks would echo followed by the shot guns. It may appear strange to those who know my love of stillness and my hatred of loud and disturbing noises that I should remember this with pleasure, but the sound of shooting in the woods, either at this time of the pheasant shoots, or when one heard the single shots of the gamekeeper on his rounds, was a seasonal sound. It was part of the country scene, and not an intrusion, going with such sights as the gamekeeper on his rounds with his gun, his dog, and his game bag.

Later on when all the leaves had gone, the fields were brown with the autumn ploughing, drilling and harrowing, and the pastures had taken on the green of winter. Then one saw great flocks of finches on the ploughlands and one could hear the crying of partridges, a curious long-drawn cry, 'Kee-eek'. Later, as spring approached, it would become the crowing of the cock bird, 'Cock-cock-a-cock-cock-a-cock-cock!', quite unlike the sound of the pheasant. One often saw pheasants singly, especially the cock pheasant with his splendid green head with scarlet wattles and white collar; but the partridges went in small flocks or coveys, and they were given to flying low across the ploughed fields with a great whirring of wings, crossing a hedge or a fence so closely that they almost seemed to touch it.

One of our pastimes in the winter was shooting with bows and arrows which we had made ourselves. A seasoned hazel or ash stick which had stood in the chimney corner for some time made a good bow. We made arrows from straight wands which we split at the top to insert a feather, afterwards binding it, and sharpening the tip at the other end.

We used to have shooting matches, with an apple on a stick stuck into the ground as a target. We stood at some distance, on opposite sides so that after one had shot an arrow the other could shoot it back, and the aim was to knock the apple down, the one who did it getting the apple; or we would stalk small birds in the hedges or rabbits in the woods and fire at them. It gave us an exciting sense of being hunters, but I cannot remember getting near enough to the quarry to do more than alarm it. In those days rabbits abounded and in the evening, especially in spring or summer, a meadow beside a wood appeared to be alive with them.

As December came, with the short, dark days, we began to sense the coming of Christmas. In this, once again, I have been fortunate, for in those days there was none of the feverish pressure of 'so many shopping days to Christmas'. Certainly we enjoyed the approach of Christmas and the feeling of anticipation, but the season had not been commercialized beyond recognition. Our Christmas was both simpler and richer than it is for most people today. One of the first signs that it was coming was when the choir started practising carols. Then we began making our Christmas cards decorated with gold and silver paint, and holly leaves, robins and snow. We spent many evenings doing this, our excitement mounting as the days got shorter and Christmas Day nearer. We did not often get much snow in those parts but soft cloudy weather such as I have already attempted to describe. With Thomas-tide the days were short and dark, but the firelight and lamplight shone warmer and more golden. We helped to stir the pudding—for a long time I thought 'Stir-Up Sunday' was the day you started to make the pudding—and the cottage was full of the smell of mince-pies and cake-making, and all manner of good things.

One day we were told that the choir was coming to sing carols in our little part of the village. We got together all the cups and mugs we possessed and made pots of tea to welcome them on the appointed evening, and then stood outside to listen. If there is any more enchanting sound than a choir singing carols at Christmastime in a remote country place I have yet to hear it. So quiet was it that we could hear them long before they reached us. Faint and far away at first, coming nearer with each stop, the immortal sounds rang across the fields and lanes. Then they had reached the shop. We could see the dark forms and the stable lanterns which they carried. Now we could hear the words, 'Once in Royal David's City', 'From Far Away We Come to You', 'Good Christian Men Rejoice', 'Good King Wenceslas', 'Oh Come! All Ye Faithful', 'We Three Kings'. We stood listening in the soft winter dark as the beautiful sounds seemed to fill the winter countryside.

Certain carols – 'Good Christian Men Rejoice', 'From Far Away We Come to You', 'God Rest Ye Merry Gentlemen' – are inseparable to me from that time and place. I can never hear them but I am back in the Sussex countryside, seeming at once so near and so far away, conscious of the fields and woods on every side under a quiet sky full of stars, hearing once more the burring Sussex voices.

When they had sung at the shop they came down to us. First they sang in the lane outside our garden gate; then we carried out the teapot and home-made buns, and everyone chattered and laughed as they drank hot tea and warmed their hands on the cups. The dark figures moved here and there in the yellow light of the lanterns, wishing us a Happy Christmas and saying 'The same to you!' when we wished them one. There was nothing but the quiet land all round and the lights from cottages and farms down in the valley; not a sound but the sudden 'Kwick! Kwick!' of a barn owl near the stables. Then they moved on and once again we heard the carols faint and far away down in the valley.

On Christmas Eve we were persuaded to go to bed in reasonable time, being assured that 'Christmas Day will come all the quicker if you go to sleep!' We hung our stockings up and eventually first we and then the older ones were fast asleep. We woke in the dark of the winter morning and felt our stockings, full of all sorts of bulges. Eventually candles were lit and we were able to pull the things out on to our beds. We had our traditions about what was put in our stockings. There was always an apple, an orange, some nuts, probably some small bags of sweets or a bag of chocolate money, some little toys, possibly a small doll for a girl and a little railway engine for a boy, some pennies, and always one present wrapped up and laid on the bed by the stocking. Part of the ritual was that we ate the apple or the orange, or both, at once, and I have always felt that an orange eaten by the light of a candle on Christmas morning tastes quite different from an orange at any other time.

Eventually we had to get dressed and ready for breakfast, and then came the walk to church. The church was decorated with holly and evergreens, and there were more carols and more smiles and 'Merry Christmases'. After we reached home we would eat Christmas dinner, usually much later than ordinary Sunday dinner. An uncle nearly always gave us a turkey which was roasted and served with bread sauce, stuffing, roast potatoes and brussel sprouts. Then there was Christmas pudding and mince-pies, if you could eat them, and then fruit, nuts and preserved ginger and crystallized fruits and chocolates. The table was gay with crackers and the dessert was accompanied by the pulling of crackers, reading of their mottoes and paper hats to wear.

At last the dinner was cleared away, and then came presents. These were always piled up on a table and covered with a cloth, so that the presents were seen as humps and bumps and craggy shapes. My father would stand at the table and pull out the presents one by one, reading out the names as each came to light. By the time this ceremony was over we were all warm, well fed and sleepy. The older ones would probably retire for forty winks while the children looked at their presents and probably started to read one of the books or look at the pictures. Eventually there was tea by the fire and at last, bed, to which we retired in a happy stupor, clutching a book or a toy of some sort.

It may sound as though this was the usual 'eat, drink and be merry' Christmas, but in fact it was not. Christmas has always been to me not only such a time as I have attempted to describe, a happy, family time, but a religious time, I would say a holy time, a time which is charged with a mystical intensity. When my father read to us, or when we heard in Church, those words from St Matthew, 'Now the birth of Jesus Christ was on this wise', or from St Luke, 'And there were in the same country shepherds abiding in the field, keeping watch over their flock by night', I was aware of the winter countryside stretching away all around us; of the stable, such a stable as I knew well, with the winter woods and the great winter sky full of stars and one bright star right over the stable itself. Outside was the ringing silence of the winter night, inside the warm yellow light of a lantern and the sound of farm animals rustling and moving in the straw.

Of all those who have painted the Nativity I believe the Flemings and the Germans have come closest to reality for me, in such pictures as Pieter Brueghel's *Nativity in the Snow*, or one painting by a Flemish painter showing just such a stable as I knew and, through a window, a bare hillside with tiny figures of shepherds and their sheep, with the twinkling of a fire and from above the unearthly light of the angel host. It is no doubt because of my upbringing and the fact that I am a northern painter, but Christmas is always a northern scene for me, German, Scandinavian, Flemish, English, and these northern paintings convey the spirit of the season more poignantly than any Italian masterpiece.

I suppose if they were asked which English writer has best evoked the spirit of Christmas the great majority of people would answer 'Dickens'. That is certainly true of one aspect of Christmas; but to me the writer who has conveyed the mystical aspect and that most intimately related to our rural tradition is Thomas Hardy. In his festival scenes he has evoked the atmosphere of a country Christmas more powerfully than any other writer; but he has also conveyed the sense of mystical unity with our countryside as no one else has done, in 'The Oxen', for example.

> Christmas Eve, and twelve of the clock,
>   Now they are all on their knees,
> An elder said as we sat in a flock
>   By the embers in hearthside ease . . .
>
> If someone said on Christmas Eve
>   'Come; see the oxen kneel
>
> 'In the lonely barton by yonder coomb
>   Our childhood used to know,'

I should go with him in the gloom
Hoping it might be so.

I feel with Christmas as with the primroses that the ecstasy is too great, the emotion too intense, to be endured for long without loss; and it is perhaps for that reason that I have a peculiar fondness for Boxing Day and for that curious week which follows, a week unlike any other week in the year, a time of slack current almost as though not life but progress is suspended. It is rather like the time of intense stillness after the bustle of harvest when the fields lie empty and at rest before ploughing begins.

On Boxing Day morning everyone gets up rather late. The air is cold and still; the newly-lit fire crackles in the grate and we enjoy a plain breakfast, perhaps of no more than toast and coffee; and then we go out into a still, cold morning to walk, or to play with newly acquired toys, or merely down to the woods to gather dead branches or fir cones for the fire. Midday dinner has its special kind of atmosphere, cold turkey, cold bread sauce, bread and butter, crystallized fruits, perhaps some bread and cheese and a cup of coffee. Then more exercise for the young and energetic, and tea by the fire warm and comfortable after the still, grey cold outside. We may read our new books and look at our presents, or we may play 'Animal Grab' or 'Snap', or perhaps my father will read to us.

I remember one book which he read to us by the fire. It was a cowboy book by Zane Grey, called *Under the Light of Western Stars*. I remember it as an exciting book, especially for two things: my father's remarkable rendering of cowboy twang and the last words, 'It is I, Majesty, your wife.' My father finished on that dramatic note, paused for a moment, and shut the book.

My father was a parson of the Church of England, although at that time he had no parish but was clerical secretary to one of the missionary societies. His mother was a farmer's daughter and she and my grandfather, also a parson, were married at her village church not far from our part of Sussex in May 1857. I remember my uncle telling me that his aunt had an urge to return to her native place to die when she grew old; as an animal will respond to an old instinct. I have often felt that it is from that source that I inherited my passion for that one region. It was not an acquired thing; it was in my blood.

My father had a beautiful voice and one of my memories of Christmastime is of him reading the opening words of the Gospel according to St John.

> 'In the beginning was the Word, and the Word was with God, and the Word was God . . .
> In Him was life; and the life was the light of men.
> And the light shineth in darkness; and the darkness comprehended it not.
> There was a man sent from God, whose name was John . . .
> He was not that Light, but was sent to bear witness of that Light.
> That was the true Light, which lighteth every man that cometh into the world.'

I am told that young people today do not understand the language of the King James Bible, but I find that hard to believe. Whenever I hear such words I feel myself back in church on a winter evening. Inside is warmth and a golden light of lamps; outside it is cold and dark, and the windows look black against the night. When I was a very small boy I would lean against my mother in the pew. She had a fur coat and I liked to feel the fur soft against my face. I felt warm and safe in the golden light with the sound of such words in my ears.

'O Ye Frost and Cold'

ONE of the things that I liked best at morning service on Sunday was when we sang the canticle, 'Benedicite, Omnia Opera' – 'O all ye Works of the Lord, bless ye the Lord: praise him, and magnify him for ever.' I would wait for special verses –'O ye Sun, and Moon', 'O ye Stars of Heaven', 'O ye Showers and Dew'; 'O ye Winter and Summer', 'O ye Frost and Cold', 'O all ye Green Things upon the Earth' – and then I would sing them with feelings of delight going up and down my spine.

We used to have family prayers in the morning, and there were certain passages in the prayers which my father read for which I always waited. He would pray 'For those labouring in the mission field', and there was one prayer which fascinated me. The only words which I can remember are – 'Travancore and Cochin and the fields of snow and ice'. When my father read those words I always saw fields, such as I knew, with hedges round them and they were piled full of snow and ice up to the tops of the hedges.

Among other things which my father read were constant references to 'the soul'. Whether it derived from some picture which I had seen I do not know, but I always saw 'the soul' as a blue object which radiated light and looked like a rolled mattress or a blue Swiss roll floating or suspended in the air.

I did not particularly like being cold but I loved the winter. I have quite often heard people nowadays say that my paintings of winter are my best, and certainly it is true that bare trees and hedges, ploughed fields and winter woods do give me intense pleasure. I remember one winter morning when I must have been a very small boy; it was the first time that I can recall being aware of frost. It was a very cold, rimy morning with a thick mist, which was clearing as the sun rose. Looking west the mist was blue and cold, but looking towards the east there was a yellowness as the sun rose. This broadened into a pale, brilliant gold, and then the sun broke through to reveal elm trees covered thick with hoar frost as dense as foliage in summer. The golden light of the sun shone on the hoary tops of the trees so that they loomed up above the mist, a brilliant, pale gold which glittered and sparkled as the frost began to melt. The grass in the meadow where I stood was stiff with frost, and I remember crunching it with my boots as I walked. Every twig in the hedgerows was covered with rime, and the scarlet hips and purple-red haws looked like candied fruit. As the mist cleared the sky was a beautiful blue streaked with golden vapour. The hedges were full of sparrows and finches which kept up a constant twittering, and as the rooks flew over to the plough-lands their cawing and the crowing of the cocks in the farm-yards came over the air with a diffused sound.

In one of my books there was a story about Jack Frost, who painted ferns and flowers in ice on the glass of the windows. On cold, frosty mornings our windows were painted in just such a way but I was never quick enough to catch Jack Frost at it. In the picture in my book he was a scraggy-looking figure with very long, thin fingers, in which he held a long brush and a pot of frost paint. I hoped I would see him, the paintings which he did on our windows were very beautiful.

After a heavy fall of snow in the night, I would wake up wondering what the strange light was on the ceiling of the bedroom, and if I scrambled out of bed I could see from the window the whole countryside looking beautiful under a thick blanket of white snow which made the hedges and the trunks of the trees look purply black. After breakfast we would throw crumbs out for the birds, which came flocking down. There was the robin, looking exactly like a picture of a robin, standing on a flower pot and singing little trills of song to thank us for the food.

The woods were particularly beautiful in snow, which made the trunks and branches of the trees look very dark, black and purple, and deep brown and tawny coloured on the ground, where dead leaves and grasses showed. The stream ran swiftly when it was full after winter rains, looking inky black against the white banks where the water was deep. If there had been a hard frost there might be sheets of ice in the slower running parts under which the water writhed and twisted. Where a fallen tree or an accumulation of leaves and branches held the snow, the water made a hollow thundering sound as though it were in a cavern.

In every direction one could see the tracks of birds and animals; moorhens' feet patterned the banks of the stream, and the starry marks of birds' feet were everywhere. Near the banks were the tracks of rabbits and across wider spaces the marks of hares, and I might see where a fox had been dragging his brush in the snow.

The cold made the birds and animals tamer than usual. They seemed to be so preoccupied with searching for food that they lost their usual fear of a human form. The blackbirds made a surprisingly loud noise as they hopped among dead leaves beneath an overhanging bank, throwing the leaves aside in a search for anything edible, and if one moved quietly one might see the little, wicked, triangular face of a weasel as he reared up behind a tuft of grass.

In later years when I came to know the paintings of Pieter Brueghel I was greatly impressed by the acuteness of his observation – he noticed and recorded with such obvious pleasure the things which I had seen so often. In his painting, *Hunters Returning in the Snow*, he has depicted the bare trees and hedges with an intimacy, an inner knowledge, which very few painters have achieved. On the left of this picture there is a fire burning, the red and gold of the flames having the effect of something mystical, the warmth and colour of the fire contrasting with the bitter cold and the snow, and conveying a sense of something ancient and symbolic as though he was aware, as I am sure he was, of the forces of light and warmth striving with those of cold and dark: the old, old struggle, as old as human life and belonging to ancient inherited instincts and memories.

This was a sight that I knew very well when the hedge-cutters were burning the trimmings. One other thing that I have often seen in nature and found recorded in his paintings is the behaviour of birds in severe weather: the way, for instance, that a crow will sit high among the bare spiky branches of a tree against a dark snow-laden sky, quite still and silent, an expression of the intense cold.

One of the most beautiful sights, which only occurred in certain conditions, was a silver thaw. If there came a bitter, freezing night after a slight thaw, in the morning the trunks and branches of the trees, even the tiniest twigs, were covered with a casing of ice. On a fine morning after such a night, when the sun broke through the mist, the thousands of twigs and branches covered with ice shone with such brilliance against the blue sky that it was almost impossible to look at them, and if there came a slight breeze the twigs clashed together with a sound like tinkling glass.

During the day the sunshine might be bright, even warm, but as the dusk fell over the winter landscape the frost descended like an unseen force, a giant hand. The wooded hills were dark against the sky and the stars appeared one by one. In the north and east the sky was clear, bright green like a bird's egg. In the west, after the red frosty disc of the sun had disappeared behind the hills, the sky was brilliant rose and gold with single stars like blazing jewels. The lights of home had a warm welcoming look towards which I plodded through the snowy lanes, thinking of hot food, steaming cups of tea and glowing fires, with the curtains drawn, the lamp-light warm and comfortable and all secure. Before going to bed after such a lamplit evening, I loved to step outside the door and see the hills dark and silent, under a great vault of clear winter sky studded with millions of brilliant stars that twinkled and almost seemed to crackle in the frost.

In those days I had not read Hardy's poems, but when in later life I came to read his lines, 'They stand at the door watching the full starred heavens that winter sees', it was these brilliant winter nights of which I thought.

Beautiful though the forms of summer are there is a special bare beauty in winter; a beauty of spiky forms, of the greys and yellows of dead grasses and the bleached angular stalks of dead cow-parsley, red docks and plants which had been foaming masses of flowers in the summer. I think this is the essential difference. One might say that in the spring, wherever one looks there are small spots and stars of flowers; in the summer the trees and the flowers are full, rounded masses; but in the winter the forms are sharp, angular, the colours as bleak and bare as the forms. Even the meadows are winter green and cold where in spring and summer they had been lush and deep. It is a sparse, bare beauty, the perfect contrast to the leafy, blossomy time. I would not be without that bare beauty, nor would I miss the way in which the stars twinkle behind bare trees on a frosty night.

Common Events and Pleasures

OUR pleasures may appear simple to those accustomed to the speed and noise of modern entertainments, yet I cannot remember a feeling at that time of having nothing to do; the days were not long enough. These simple pleasures have stayed with me as a sweet taste in the mouth, like heather honey lying upon the tongue. An 'outing' meant so much; not just because it was a rare occurrence but because of the richness of its texture.

A really important occasion was a journey to the sea twelve miles away, by the carrier's cart. This was a large, hooded wagon pulled by two draught horses, with a bench on both sides for passengers and room for luggage as well. It was owned by the blacksmith, who lived at the opposite end of the village, near the Place, by a little green where the inn stood. He worked the forge, ran the carrier business and probably did some farming as well with his two sons. The wagon went past us once a week early in the morning, returning in the evening, to be met at the bottom of our steep hill by one of the sons with an extra horse for the pull up. It was quite a sight to see the three fine horses hauling it past our gate.

If we were going on such an outing it meant a very early start. We felt a peculiar sense of excitement while waiting in the sharpness of the early morning air, after a very early breakfast, for the wagon to arrive. I recall one particular morning, grey and still with a thick, nebulous mist lying over the valley below, not a sound to be heard but the bark of a dog or the lowing of cows and the clatter of buckets from the cowshed near by. We asked Mr Farmer if it was going to be a nice day. 'Oh ah!', he said, 'It'll be warm just na'ow when the mist clears.' The grass verge was heavy and grey with dew, the trees were grey-green phantom shapes. Then we heard the sound of the horses' hooves and the rumbling of the wheels as the wagon came into sight. There were two or three of us, several people already on the benches and a couple to pick up at the bottom of the hill.

Down by the bridge in a meadow Mrs Whitehouse of the farm kept a great many ducks. 'Er ducks do grow!' said a woman on the bench. It is strange how that remark sounds in my mind as clear today as though I had recorded it. How many years ago was that on a grey morning before a hot day? Yet I hear it now with the very turn and inflexion of the voice that spoke.

Mr Farmer was right: the mist lifted and cleared, the sun broke through and it was one of those splendid days, those incredible days, when the sky was cloudless, like a great blue bowl resting upon the horizon. It was a hilly journey, hard work for the horses. About a couple of miles along the valley we came to a crossroad called the Hole; there we turned to the left to climb a long hill. After the top was reached we came to another village, where we turned to the right. For a while the going was easier until we approached another hill, which we always called the Wall because as you approached along a straight piece of road it seemed to stand straight up in front of you. Here most of us got out to lessen the load, and we were glad of a stretch as we climbed the hill.

It was a slow steady plodding journey with the rumble of the wheels, the swaying of the canvas hood, the sound of the horses' feet; a journey in which every moment counted. There was no feeling of impatience or frustration, no worrying about 'When do we get there'; we were 'there' all the time. The journey lives as a whole, with our eventual arrival at the sea with the sparkling water, the sound of the waves, the strong smell of salt and fish, the crying of the gulls, being parts of a perfect whole. I do not remember any entertainments or raucous funfair. I remember little shops with the doors festooned with buckets and spades and shrimping nets; inside were sticks of rock and coloured picture-postcards (some of them very vulgar); mirrors stuck all over with sea-shells; pictures or flowers or coloured stars in paperweights made of thick glass; jugs, teapots and dishes for jam with 'A present from . . .' written on them; little weather houses in which the man came out with an umbrella when it was wet and the woman with a sun bonnet when it was fine; and snowstorms in glass balls. You tipped these upside down, and when you put them right way up again the snow fell thickly and settled on the people or animals or houses in the scene.

Down on the beach the sun was hot; food tasted like celestial fare; bathing, paddling or wandering among the rocks and pools was the pinnacle of human enjoyment. All day long the sun beat down, and our ears were full of the sound of the waves, the shouting of the boatmen taking people for trips on the sea, the crying of the gulls. But at length the sun began to go down in the western sky, the light became more golden, the heat less intense and it was time to find the carrier's cart. It was sad, of course, to leave the sea. As the tide went out there were great stretches of sand, with rocks and pools and piles of seaweed where there had been water. I wished I could stay and use the shrimping nets to search for shells and seaweed and crabs as other children were doing who were staying there. Yet, in a sense, there was still a pleasant feeling of anticipation; these were things that I would do one day.

The long rumbling journey home, over twelve miles of country road, ever deeper and deeper among the lanes and woods, brought us home at last, tired, sunburnt, smelling of sea and sand and carrying a bucketful of shells and long swathes of seaweed and even, at the bottom, some real sea-water. We ate our supper in a drowsy half-stupor of blessed tiredness; and then came deep, dreamless sleep.

We had other entertainments. Sometimes there were shows at the village hall. I remember the visit of a travelling concert party who burlesqued *East Lynne*. 'Ah, Willie, after walking many weary miles –.' 'Why didn't you take a train!' Roars of laughter. And there was a skit on a curate, which we tried not to laugh at, because we shouldn't really. 'Next Monday there will be a meeting of the Boys' Club; I shall not be there. On Wednesday the Girls' Club will meet; I *shall* be there!' 'The

preachers for next Sunday will be found hanging in the porch.'
And a kind of refrain, 'I *like* it — I *like* it! It's very nice to be — a
simple country Curate — with a weakness for his tea!'

We should not have laughted of course, but it was hard not
to; and there was one bit when Willie was going to bed and he
looked under the bed to see if the necessary article was there.
This produced cat-calls and stamping applause from some of
the lads; we were very simple in those days.

There was one quite dreadful occasion when two girls whom
we knew went to a village hop — in pyjamas! I imagine they were
more respectable than many modern dresses; but it caused
quite a stir. On another occasion the school children put on an
entertainment in which, my memory tells me, some of the items
were a little unsuitable. ''Ark! Oi 'ear moi nursey callin'' did
sound a trifle odd in those days, all spoken in a beautiful Sussex
burr by children who probably had only the vaguest ideas of
what it was about. There was a diversion, on this occasion,
caused by a visiting child with a high, screaming, London
voice. She took part in the sketch but was star-gazing and
missed her cue. Then came a pause; everyone looked ex-
pectantly at her but nothing happened, then someone gave her a
nudge. The result was so startling that I can never forget it.
After the low-toned, rounded phrasing of the country children
the shrill Cockney voice burst out with a shattering effect: 'Yes,
I heard her as she flew on the wings of the evening breeze!'

A great event was the tennis tournament when all 'the
County' foregathered in the park. The village children attended
to field stray balls. The girls wore white dresses, white hats and
white stockings, mostly of a fairly haphazard style and fit. It was
a tremendous occasion on which the children were paid so
much and given a free tea. Sometimes there was a fête up at the
Hall in aid of some charity or mission. I remember one fête on a
very hot day when my sister and I were given a large strawberry
ice made of real cream; an unforgettable event. At this same fête
there was a very pretty lively Finnish girl who was staying at a
local rectory. There was also a man of vaguely military
appearance with waxed moustaches. Who he was I do not
know, but his rather dashing manner towards the Finnish girl
was considered 'not quite nice'.

The Rector sang a song, 'Love Will Find Out a Way', and a lady played a mandolin, which I thought very fine. Ever since reading *The Secret Garden* I had wanted to play a musical instrument. I saw myself as Dickon, charming rabbits and squirrels with my pipe. I even acquired a tin flageolet, but the only tune that I could play was a halting rendering of 'Three Blind Mice'.

Conclusion

Now I have sat by my fire, staring at the flames and remembering many things. As I have remembered and as the pictures have flashed across my mind I have jotted them down in a medium which is not my own: in words. I have made no attempt to do what I am not equipped to do, to write a story, or to conceive and present a plot, for I am a painter, not a writer, I cannot think in terms of words but only in terms of images. So I have allowed myself to ramble, to string things together as best I can.

If in assembling these random notes and sketches I have awakened memories in others who have known them as I have done, I have achieved all I can hope for. It may seem to younger people that I am getting old, that things are no longer precise, that I wander in a haze. This may well be true; but I should like to think that some younger ones will gain pleasure out of what I have written. If my scribblings give them a tenth part of the pleasure that remembering has given me then I have not entirely failed.

So many happy memories come back to me like a flock of plovers turning and twisting in wonderful flight, the sunlight flashing on their wings as they wheel in a twinkling throng. Can everything have been so enchanted? By enchantment I do not mean an unnatural bewitchment: yet it is an enchantment, filled with the beauty of natural things; shining with the radiance of a clear evening in May; of the earth, earthy.

A Morning without Clouds

As I look back at my remembered landscape it shines, not with an unearthly but with an earthy radiance, 'in clear shining after rain' . . .